# A quarter century
# on the road to stardom

## by John Zimmermann

# THE HERITAGE CONTINUES.

When Yokohama developed a replacement for its legendary A008RS we didn't stretch the envelope, we put it in the shredder.

 The A032R is a direct descendant of our IMSA racing tires with new casing, sidewall and tread compounding that last longer and corner harder with wet traction that blows the competition off the track. If a picture is worth a thousand words, this tire speaks volumes. Tread blocks that don't know the meaning of the word squirm, Aqua Tusk channels that move more water than the Hoover Dam, all in a DOT-approved package that you can take to the street, quickly.

## ⟫⟫ YOKOHAMA

### TURN ON TECHNOLOGY™

< 5 >

For information or additional copies:

55 Monument Circle, Suite 400
Indianapolis, IN  46204

P(317) 684-9900
F(317) 684-9800

Content & direction: John Zimmermann
Photography compilation & editing: Paul Webb

Special thanks to the all the talented photographers who contributed to this book: Cheryl Day Anderson, Kenneth Andersen,
Allen Beaulieu, Dan Boyd, Art Flores, Ron Hussey, Susan Majoy, Paul Strak, Monika Strak, Marc Sproule,
Chris Waddell, Paul Webb, Mark Weber and John Zimmermann.
Jacques Villenueve 1993 pic courtesy of Player's Library.


A very special thanks to the efforts of Paul Webb, Marc Sproule, and Paul and Monika Strak of Gridwork.
Without their help and wonderful photo archives this book would not have been possible.




Graphic design by Waypoint, Brussels
Color separation by Dataflash, Belgium
Printed in Belgium by EDP Européenne De Presse sa  - Fleurus

< 5 >

Draft.

Go inside.

Never look back.

Nothing but open pavement

and another corner.

Stay focused.

160 mph.

Everything's a blur.

Stay focused.

But it sure is cool,

'cause when you pass 'em

all they see is a brilliant

flash of color.

Stay focused.

MCI
YOKOHAMA

There's no "I" in team.

But there is in winner.

**TOYOTA** *motor sports*

# TABLE OF CONTENTS

| 8 | Foreword |
|---|---|
| 12 | Introduction |
| 16 | A Quarter Century on the Road to Stardom |
| 80 | Gordon Kirby's Top-Ten Atlantic Graduates |
| 84 | Vicki O'Connor Racer's wife to Series President |
| 88 | Oh Canada! |
| 94 | Looking Back A Veteran's View |
| 100 | The 1997 Championship |
| 200 | Looking Ahead - Vicki O'Connor |

< 7 >

# FOREWORD

Foreword
>           Atlantic's Number One Son
Introduction
>           Vicki O'Connor
>           Gerald R. Forsythe
A Quarter Century
>           In the Beginning
>           Brother Jacques' Turn
>           Tires: The Essential Ingredient
>           Salvaging the Series
>           The Third Era Dawns
Gordon Kirby
Vicki O'Connor
Oh Canada
>           Grand Prix of Montreal
>           Grand Prix of Trois Rivières
Looking Back
1997 Championship
>           Introduction
>           The Teams
>           The Drivers
>           Nowhere without the Teams
>           1997 Season's Review
>           1997 Final Standings
>           1997 K(O)L Toyota Awards
Looking Ahead
>           One Make for the Future
>           Vicki O'Connor

< 9 >

# Atlantic's Number One Son
## Jacques Villeneuve

My first race in Atlantic was in 1992 at Trois-Rivières, and racing for the first time at that historic event was very important for me. It also was very special to win the following year in front of the home crowd in Montreal. The Atlantic series was born in Canada, and it has been and still is a very important element of the Canadian driver development program. I'm proud of my Canadian heritage and of the fact that I got my start there.

I have many great memories of the time I spent in the Atlantic series. I feel that it is an excellent step in the racing ladder, and the best series in North America to prepare a driver for Indy cars. I spent just one full year in Atlantic, in 1993, but it was a critical year in my career. Not only had I moved to a more professional and competitive series, but I also began my association with Player's, and Barry Green. Before that I had been racing in Japan, and the Atlantic series got me a lot of exposure at home in Canada and in North America. Everyone learned to work together as a team at that level, and it helped to prepare me for the move up to Indy cars in 1994. The following year we won the CART championship.

I think the biggest benefit to driving the Atlantic car is the ground effects and learning to adapt to the downforce they generate. You go from that to an Indy car, and the feeling is very much the same. The Indy car is just a little bigger and a lot faster! Also, driving in Atlantic taught me the value and discipline of working with an experienced engineer to set up the car for different types of tracks, like road courses, street courses and ovals. The very close competition in 1993, especially the duels with David Empringham and with my teammate Claude Bourbonnais, really helped to prepare me for the highly competitive fields in Indy cars and Formula One.

In a way, my own interest in racing cars began with the Atlantic series. I was a boy, and I remember growing up in that atmosphere. My father launched his career by winning the Atlantic championship. His accomplishments, and those of my uncle Jacques, mean a lot to the people of Canada, and they helped give birth to the tradition of great Canadian drivers. I'm proud to be able to carry on that tradition.

I still follow the Atlantic series when I can. Last year at the Grand Prix in Montreal, when Bertrand Godin won the Atlantic race for Player's, I watched the race from the Williams pit. It shows that the legacy of Atlantic is alive and well!

I wish Vicki and the series all the best for the next 25 years, and good luck to the rising stars who chose this path to success.

Sincerely,

Jacques Villeneuve

< 11 >

# INTRODUCTION

Foreword
        Atlantic's Number One Son
Introduction
        Vicki O'Connor
        Gerald R. Forsythe
A Quarter Century
        In the Beginning
        Brother Jacques' Turn
        Tires: The Essential Ingredient
        Salvaging the Series
        The Hard-Era Dawns
Gordon Kirby
Vicki O'Connor
Oh Canada
        Grand Prix of Montreal
        Grand Prix at Trois Rivieres
Looking Back
1997 Championship
        Introduction
        The Teams
        The Drivers
        Nowhere without the Teams
        1997 Season's Review
        1997 Final Standings
        1997 KOOL Toyota Awards
Looking Ahead
        One Make for the Future
        Vicki O'Connor

< 13 >

I'm really very proud to see the history of the 25 years of Atlantic racing in print.

I count myself lucky that my life has followed the Atlantic series so closely from its birth and throughout its growth. In its heydey, when it was called the Player's Challenge Series in Canada in the '70s, I traveled to every race with my husband Bill, who was racing in the series. Atlantic was so popular then that we had qualifying races to make the final grid. Player's had TV coverage on CTV's Wide World of Sports. They were way ahead of their time.

I also was there through the leanest years. When I came on board as organizer in 1985, we had five races, maybe 15 cars, a $5000 purse and absolutely no TV coverage. With the help of Player's and a lot of friends — especially the teams that stuck with us and fielded cars when times were tough -- we were able to bring the series back to life. Then, with the arrival of Toyota as the series title sponsor in 1989, and associate sponsors, Yokohama Tire and TRD, and now with Brown & Williamson's KOOL brand, as well as Player's sponsorship of the Player's Challenge in the Canadian races, we have reached the growth and prosperity we see today. These corporations had a lot of belief in us. As a result, we are living the glory years right now.

Without the tireless efforts of all these people, Atlantic may not have survived these 25 years. I think Atlantic has attracted that level of faith and support because there has always been something about these cars -- and their drivers -- that has endeared them to us. The sound of the Atlantic engine says it all: fast, sexy, violent, hard-charging -- all the things that excite the drivers, the team members and the fans. And we are fortunate to know the drivers when they are still on their way up. I'm always sad to see them graduate from our family, but our purpose is to help them move on. We have produced a long list of well-known graduates. Even though they went on to become champions in other forms of racing, they all remember fondly their days with us.

Luckily, the friendships made in Atlantic outlast all others. One of the neatest things about this series is that, despite its growth and the growth of motorsports as a whole, the friendly, fun-loving atmosphere remains unchanged.

That atmosphere has produced many great stories, and I am sure that if you were a part of this history, you will remember many of your own as you read this book. If not, I hope you enjoy reading this history as much as I and all of my friends have enjoyed living it.

Best wishes,

Vicki O'Connor
President, Pro-Motion Agency, Ltd.

It gives me great pleasure to introduce to you this book commemorating the 25th Anniversary of the KOOL/Toyota Atlantic Series.

Twenty-five years ago, Canada's Player's Challenge Series for Formula B cars was opened to international competitors and introduced one of the finest powerplants in the history of racing, the Cosworth BDA. At the same time the series was renamed Formula Atlantic, a name that today is recognized worldwide as the most productive, competitive and cost-effective developmental racing series in the world for both drivers and teams.

With a long history of stellar talent and fantastic racing, Atlantic nevertheless encountered growing pains along the way. Then in 1989, Toyota Motor Sales USA entered the picture.Seizing the opportunity to join forces with a tremendous grass-roots racing series while focusing a spotlight on its incredibly powerful, compact and reliable 4A-GE four-cylinder engine, Toyota stepped up and committed its vast resources to stabilizing, promoting and growing the Championship.

In 1993, Player's Ltd. Of Canada capitalized on its long association with Atlantic by becoming title co-sponsor, which resulted in a tremendous increase in the prestige, prize money and media exposure provided to the competitors. As many of you no doubt know, my association with the Atlantic series began this same year when I teamed with Player's to bring the current Formula One World Champion, Jacques Villeneuve, to North America to race Atlantics. Building from that experience base, he graduated to CART, winning the Rookie of the Year in 1994 and the PPG CART World Series Championship in 1995. I am very proud of our role in helping Villeneuve reach the top.

Villeneuve's story is an important one. It demonstrates to the world the value of the Atlantic series as a training ground for future champions. It also demonstrates the tremendous importance of having a well-funded, systematic driver development structure such as the one Player's has established in Canada.

I believe that here in the United States, we have made great strides in refining and defining our ladder to the top. However, as motorsports becomes increasingly international in its reach, the competitiveness of the top series increases. We have seen this in the tremendous show put on by CART in the last few seasons. In order to prepare drivers to face these mounting challenges, we have more work to do.

When I acquired the Atlantic series from Vicki O'Connor in August of 1996, our goal was to establish a secure, long term future for this important platform. My desire is for Atlantic cars to play an increasingly important role in rearing new talent, so that we can be assured of a future generation of household names on par with Andretti, Rahal, Unser, Vasser and Villeneuve.

Now with major commitments from KOOL, Toyota and Player's, along with significant contributions from Yokohama Tires, BBS Wheels, Bosch Spark Plugs, MCI, TRD, Swift Engineering and other associates, the KOOL/Toyota Atlantic Championship promises to bring competitors and fans from all over the world together to experience the richest and most competitive development series in auto racing for many years to come.

This book illustrates in beautiful detail the role Atlantic has played in producing the stars of the past and present. I'm looking forward to the challenge and opportunity of guiding that historic effort in the years to come.

Sincerely,

Gerald R. Forsythe

< 15 >

Foreword
     Atlanta's Number One Son
Introduction
     Vicki O'Connor
     Gerald R. Forsythe
A Quarter Century
     In the Beginning
     Brcitin/Jacques Toro
     Tires: The Essential Ingredient
     Salvaging the Series
     The Third Era Dawns
Gordon Kirby
Vicki O'Connor
Oh Canada
     Grand Prix of Montreal
     Grand Prix of Trois-Rivieres
Looking Back
1997 Championship
     Introduction
     The Teams
     The Drivers
     Nowhere without the Teams
     1997 Season's Review
     1997 Final Standings
     1997 KOOL Toyota Awards
Looking Ahead
     One Make for the Future
     Vicki O'Connor

< 17 >

## 25 Years as Racing's
## Most Prolific Training Category

The KOOL/Toyota Atlantic Championship celebrates its silver anniversary season in 1998, having prospered over those 25 years by encouraging the myth and magic of every racing driver's dream, while offering a proper training ground for and steppingstone to that goal. Throughout that quarter of a century, Atlantic has done this by promoting a nimble, well-balanced racing car in which young drivers could learn the basics of the craft at the highest possible level.

This instruction comes not only on the track, fighting against others chasing the same dream, but also in the pits, where can be absorbed the art of communication with racing cars through chassis adjustments, gear selection and the like, and the paddock, where seminars in sponsorship and presentation are readily available to those willing to become full-fledged professionals. Atlantic races have traditionally been all-out sprints of between 60 and 100 miles, and – except for those run on oval tracks – have always begun with one of the most exciting spectacles in all of racing, the standing start.

As it marks this landmark season as North American racing's most productive single-seat training category, the Atlantic formula enjoys perhaps its greatest popularity ever. Thanks to the support of Brown and Williamson Tobacco's KOOL brand, Toyota Motor Sales USA, Player's and tire supplier Yokohama, purses have never been larger, starting grids regularly average more than 30 cars, each year's champion earns a test session in a CART championship car courtesy of Toyota and every race in the championship is televised on espn2.

Yesterday...

...and today.

Alex Barron's championship
earned a day at the wheel of
the Toyota Champ car

< 19 >

Eventual series owner Bill O'Connor and his teammate
Tom Klausler duke it out at Watkins Glen in '73

Atlantic's history of making names and establishing careers may reach back 25 years, but the origins of the basic class actually stretch even farther, to 1965, when Formula B, its direct antecedent, evolved from Formula Junior. Established for 1000lb, single-seat, open-wheel racing cars powered by 200hp, 1.6-liter, twin-cam engines, Formula B offered professional series in both the USA and Canada, eventually becoming Canada's national championship with sponsorship from Player's cigarettes.

That Player's Challenge Series ran to Formula B specifications for three years between 1971 and 1973 – crowning Jacques Couture, Brian Robertson and Bill Brack as its annual champions – before adopting Atlantic rules with the advent of the Cosworth BDA in 1974. The BDA (belt-driven A series in Cosworth parlance) was a four-valve-per cylinder development of the twin-cam conversion for Ford's ubiquitous 1600cc four-cylinder engine.

During its early years as Canada's national championship, the series built its reputation by offering drivers many benefits, not the least of which was the national television coverage given the series by an alliance with Canada's CTV network. On the Saturday following each championship contest, CTV's Wide World of Sports program presented a condensed account of the race that provided monumental exposure at a time when thoroughbred motorsport had yet to make any truly significant impact on television.

A new series develops

< 21 >

## In the beginning

It was during Atlantic's first season that Richard Nixon resigned. The 1974 schedule listed seven championship rounds at circuits in six Canadian provinces, and four non-points races, one through the streets of fabled Trois-Rivières, Quebec, and three in the USA, at Road America, Watkins Glen and the Waterford Hills track in suburban Detroit.

Driving both his own Doug Crosty-developed Lotus and a newer Chevron, Toronto auto dealer Bill Brack won four of the seven points-paying races to repeat as Player's Challenge champion, with Bill O'Connor and Tom Klausler – fielding two cars sponsored by Chicago Lola importer Carl Haas – taking two others to claim runner-up honors.

That inaugural season was also notable for two other occurrences of interest, as the non-championship season finale at Watkins Glen was won by Klausler's teammate, Bill O'Connor, husband of current series organizer Vicki O'Connor, and the debut season of a fast, young French-Canadian driver that was cut short by a crash at Mosport that broke his leg. That driver was, of course, Gilles Villeneuve.

Elliot Forbes-Robinson
Trois Rivières, Quebec - 1975

Gilles Villeneuve - Brainerd, MN. 1975

In its second season, the series began to gain momentum. Brack again emerged as champion, forced to rely on consistent performances in his STP Chevron to subdue the challenges of Swedish March driver Bertil Roos, Klausler and Elliott Forbes-Robinson, the latter two in Lolas. Running his March out of his motor home, Villeneuve surprised the veterans in the rain on the airport circuit at Gimli, Manitoba, to claim his first win in the third race of his second season.

Bill Brack - Edmonton, Alberta - 1975

Gilles Villeneuve
Brainerd, MN. - 1975

< 23 >

Gilles blossomed the following year. Dual championships were organized, with an IMSA-sanctioned U.S. series joining the CASC's Player's Challenge on the calendar to expand the Atlantic season – counting the non-points street race in Trois-Rivières, Quebec – to 13 rounds. Driving the Skiroule March for Chris Harrison's Ecurie Canada, Villeneuve won nine times from 10 starts to sweep both titles, in the process winning perhaps the most famous race in Atlantic history, that year's Grand Prix Molson Trois-Rivières. There, he faced a field enhanced for the occasion by a handful of imported Formula 1 drivers that included the soon-to-be World Champion, James Hunt, future World Champ Alan Jones, Vittorio Brambilla (who'd won at Trois-Rivières the year before) and Patrick Depailler – as well as French comingman Patrick Tambay.

Gilles handily beat them all, sending Hunt back to McLaren touting the bright young talent he'd encountered. Perhaps Lord James merely needed a good excuse for losing, but whatever the case, the next summer Villeneuve was given a test with McLaren and a start, in a third team car, for the British Grand Prix. By the end of the year he was racing for Enzo Ferrari, and the rapidity of his progression has fueled the dreams of Atlantic hopefuls ever since.

No one, before or since, could hang it out the way Gilles did.

< 25 >

Gilles Villeneuve - Quebec City, Quebec - 1977

When Canadian government tobacco regulators derailed Player's support of the series after 1976, Labatt's Breweries stepped in as title sponsor for Villeneuve's successful defense of his crown in Harrison's Direct Film March. His focus perhaps diffused by the trans-Atlantic travel required to pursue his opportunity with McLaren, Gilles won but three of the eight championship rounds – IMSA's series had vanished after a single shot – and was forced to win the final two races to fend off Bobby Rahal, Brack, Keke Rosberg and Price Cobb, each with one of the four victories he had missed.

Price Cobb

Price Cobb studies the line
with Bobby Rahal

Keke Rosberg

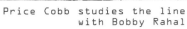

< 27 >

In 1978, with Gilles off driving Grands Prix in Ferraris, the Labatt Challenge Series assumed an Americanadian identity with races on both sides of the 49th parallel co-sanctioned by the CASC and the SCCA.  Driving March agent Doug Shierson's house car, Howdy Holmes overcame Rosberg's Fred Opert Chevron and Cobb's Ecurie Canada March for the crown.  Also recorded that year was the first of many victories for the formula's most dominant carmaker, Ralt, as Rahal won at Lime Rock in Pierre Phillips' Red Roof Inns RT-1.

Howdy Holmes - Hamilton, Ontario - 1978

< 29 >

Trois Rivières, Quebec - 1978

Bobby Rahal leads
Keke Rosberg and Price Cobb Quebec City, Quebec - 1978

The '78 season was Rosberg's last in the series, and though he may have missed the Atlantic title, he put what he'd learned to good use in winning the 1982 World Championship for Williams. Like Rosberg, Rahal's greatest successes came after he graduated, with PPG Cup championships in 1986, '87 and '92, and his Indy 500 win in 1986. He's now an owner/driver in the PPG Cup series, embarking on his final year as a driver. Also racing in Atlantic at the time was a young Kentuckian named Danny Sullivan, and while he may never have managed much in Atlantic, he later collected the famous spin-and-win Indy 500 in '85 and a PPG Cup championship three years later.

Bobby Rahal
Quebec City, Quebec - 1978

Danny Sullivan - Hamilton, Ontario - 1978

Keke Rosberg - Montreal, Quebec - 1978

< 33 >

Ralt and March split the 1979 Atlantic season down the middle as Ralt-mounted Tom Gloy won only the Long Beach season opener but scored points everywhere to earn the crown. Defending champion Holmes and promising young Californian Kevin Cogan, in a Ralt, each won three races, while newcomer Jeff Wood took two for March and Bob Earl one for Ralt. Holmes took time off to race at Indianapolis that May, snagging Rookie of the Year honors in the annual 500-mile race, but crashed heavily at the annual Macau Grand Prix in the fall.

Bob Earl and Tim Fortner - 1979

Tom Gloy and Howdy Holmes - 1979

Kevin Cogan - 1979

1979 Champion Tom Gloy at Westwood, B.C.

Kevin Cogan leads the way
at Westwood, B.C. - 1979

< 37 >

Standing start miscue left J.V. and his #6
car going backwards while the rest of the
field went for the green at Trois-Rivières -
1980. Fortunately everyone survived the
mayhem that followed. Note onlookers

Gloy commenced his title defense in 1980 with back-to-back wins at Long Beach and Sears Point, but couldn't hold off the charge of the next Villeneuve – Gilles' younger brother Jacques – while diverting energy toward his future with a handful of PPG Cup starts for a satellite Penske operation. Those aspirations ultimately came to naught, but Gloy did become a force in the Trans-Am, claiming the series crown as a driver in 1984 and more recently fielding a competitive, multi-car, factory-assisted team. This year his team, in partnership with Rahal, will tackle NASCAR's Craftsman Truck Series.

A nip and tuck battle for the 1980 Mamiya Cameras North American Formula Atlantic Championship raged between the Quebecois and the Californian all year, settled only when Jacques swept the final two races in Montreal and Mexico City with Shierson's March. Cobb added a fifth win for March at Trois-Rivières, while Earl, Wood and Steve Saleen cut single notches in Ralt's column to go with Gloy's pair. Wood's win at Bridgehampton was particularly historic, being the first for Ralt's RT-4, the formula's first true ground-effects car. The RT-4 had debuted at Long Beach that spring, destined to become the single most successful chassis model in Atlantic history.

One sad note clouded the 1980 season, as promising newcomer Tom Stewart was killed in a practice crash at Lime Rock. Stewart, however, remains the only fatality yet recorded in professional Atlantic racing.

Tom Gloy - Long Beach, CA - 1980

J.V. at Lime Rock, CT - 1980

< 39 >

Jacques joined his brother as a repeat Atlantic champion in '81, winning four of nine races in the latest Shierson March. The remaining five victories were spread equally among RT-4 drivers Geoff Brabham – in a cameo run with the works team at Long Beach – Whitney Ganz, Tim Coconis, Mexican Rogelio Rodriguez and Cogan. Though he never managed to match his brother's F1 exploits, Jacques did go on to win the Can-Am championship in '83 and claim a PPG Cup race two years later. Cogan also moved up, signing to drive for Penske Racing the next season, and later scoring a PPG Cup victory for Patrick Racing at Phoenix in 1986.

Shierson, whose team won three Atlantic championships in nine years before eventually moving into the PPG Cup racing – and winning the 1990 Indy 500 with Arie Luyendyk – calls his years in the series "the best racing I ever did. If you look back at the caliber of drivers who were running then, and where they went on to, and how good they were, I loved the whole thing. It was very, very competitive on the race track, but we were all friends afterward. Everybody would help everybody else – except on the race track, and then we'd go for it."

Doug Shierson with
Bobby Rahal

Jacques Villeneuve at Mosport, Ontario - 1981

< 43 >

## Tires: The Essential Ingredient

No matter how wonderfully efficient or technically advanced a racing car design may be, it will never get anywhere without tires. One can very easily overlook these essential ingredients because all cars need them and have them, but every racer knows they will go nowhere fast without a proper tire.

The history of tires in Atlantic racing runs a course fairly parallel to that of the cars, for tire choice was wide open in the beginning and various tires from Goodyear, Firestone, Dunlop and others appeared on the cars. Over time, bias-ply Goodyears became the series' de facto tire choice, and for many years it was easier than usual to forget about tires because they were a constant in the equation. There was ongoing experimentation with compounds and constructions, of course, and drivers who could manage their tires properly achieved the best results, but the rubber ringing the wheels at each corner of the car was pretty much taken for granted.

In 1989, Yokohama stepped up to become the renamed Toyota Atlantic Championship's first specified tire, and Yokohama's original 13in. bias-ply tires were designed with the objective of increased longevity. "I thought the tire was acceptable in that regard," noted veteran Atlantic entrant Pierre Phillips, "but it's always dependent upon the driver; if the driver's really fast, you go through tires."

After five seasons with bias plies, Yokohama switched to radial construction for its Atlantic tires with the 1994 season, and that tire, still with a 13in. diameter, remained in use until the end of last year. For Atlantic's 25th season in 1998, however, the tiremaker is introducing an all-new 15in. radial designed specifically for the new Swift 008 a chassis that comes on the scene this year as the car of the future for the KOOL/Toyota Atlantic Championship.

One of the most closely contested seasons in series history took place in 1982. Until the championship finale at Mosport, no driver could win more than once, and even though Californian Whitney Ganz claimed both that finale and the earlier Mosport round, New Zealander Dave McMillan compiled consistent points-scoring finishes all season long with his Centerline Wheels Ralt to lock away the crown. Ralts won every race that year, as they would for the next four and a half seasons.

Dave McMillan leads Dan Marvin at Mid-Ohio - 1982

Al Unser Jr. - Long Beach, CA - 1982

Norm Hunter at Mosport, Ontario - 1982

Whitney Ganz at Mosport, Ontario - 1982

1982 title defender Dave McMillan at Riverside, CA - 1983 in the ill-fated Dart Chassis.

Michael Andretti at Willowsprings, CA - 1983

As it continued to grow, the Atlantic series managed to catch the eye of the FIA which, in 1983, tried to absorb it into a global "Formula Mondial" scheme. The plan was to have four "zone" championships – Pacific, North American, European and Asian – with the top performers from each to meet in a season-ending "world" championship run-off. The concept failed to consider Atlantic's essential locally based nature, however, and only the Pacific (Australia and New Zealand) and North American zones ever even held races, let alone crowned champions.

On the race track, the North American Zone produced the expected tight competition as Michael Andretti, in Brian Robertson's Ralt American works entry, fought off the independent shoestring operation run by Aussie Greg "Pee Wee" Siddle for talented Brazilian Roberto Moreno. Moreno won four races to Andretti's three, but missed one round and failed to score at another so that Michael outpointed him handily in the end. Later that year, Andretti ran his first PPG Cup race, and enters the 1998 season as CART's winningest active driver, his 36 victories the fourth-best tally of all time. He also won the PPG Cup in 1991 and endured a lost year of F1 in '93. While perhaps not as successful as Andretti, Moreno has also raced with distinction in both F1 and CART.

< 47 >

## Salvaging the Series

From the Mondiale mess, ironically, emerged one of Atlantic's finest hours, although it may not have seemed so at the time. The category was essentially in shambles, but was soon rescued by a band of dedicated loyalists who picked up the pieces left by the FIA and began putting them back together. WCAR, for West Coast Atlantic Racing, had first surfaced as a modest, regional subseries within the Mondiale scheme, but became the country's premier Atlantic championship by default the following year.

Those aforementioned friends of the formula, SCCA board member Jon Norman and his fellow entrants, Rick and Gudrun Shea and Tim Fortner, kept the flame burning and the dream alive by laying the foundation for what Atlantic has become today. Norman's driver, Dan Marvin – who'd run with Villeneuve and the rest as a rookie in '76 and would enjoy significant post-Atlantic success in Camel Lights prototypes – won five of '84's nine races in a Stefan Dwornik-prepared Ralt to hold off steady Chris Bender by a slim four points for the title.

Rick Shea - shown here expressing his feelings about an endlessly delayed race day at Hamilton, Ontario in 1978 - applied much the same approach in helping to put the series back on track for 1984

Michael Angus at Road Atlanta - 1985

Jeff Wood holds off Dan Marvin at Seattle, WA - 1985

WCAR's concept of affordable Atlantic racing in a geographically focused series caught on in the east as well – where Vicki O'Connor's Chicago-based Pro-Motion Agency established an ECAR clone for 1985. A total of 15 races were run nationwide in the two series. Marvin and Jeff Wood, in Alister McNeill's Ralt, each won four races in a classic duel for the Western crown from which Wood emerged, while Michael Angus won two of six races in Stuart Moore's Ralt to dominate the ECAR side of things.

Defending champion Dan Marvin
hangs it out at Westwood,
B.C. - 1985

< 49 >

Scott Goodyear at Road America, WI - 1986

The following year, Canadian Scott Goodyear revitalized his career by winning five of nine eastern rounds with Tom Mitchell's Ralt to outduel Englishman Calvin Fish for ECAR's EZ-Wider championship. In the West, California's Ted Prappas took Allan McCall's Team Tui Ralt to three wins and outpointed Mexico's Roberto Quintanilla for the title.

Ted Prappas at Firebird, AZ - 1986

The field gets under way - Montreal - 1986

< 51 >

Eventual West Coast champion Johnny
O'Connell shows Jimmy Vasser and Dean Hall
the quick way around Laguna Seca - 1987

Steve Shelton, Michael Greenfield
and Calvin Fish celebrate
a good day at Road Atlanta, GA - 1987

Scott Goodyear at Elkhart Lake, WI - 1987

Ralt's long reign of supremacy in Atlantic came to an end in 1987 with the midseason introduction of the California-built Swift DB4. Steve Shelton debuted the prototype DB4 at Watkins Glen in July, but the model's first victory didn't come until September in Portland in the hands of series debutante R.K. Smith. The championships east and west still fell to Ralt drivers, however, as Calvin Fish won three races in Bill O'Connor's Comprep RT-4 to prevail in the East's HFC Pro Series, and Johnny O'Connell, driving the McNeill Motorsports RT-4, won four times to defeat Dean Hall for the Stefan Petroff Industries-backed western championship. Smith also won the first great head-to-head shootout between East and West at Memphis, a vibrant precursor of things to come.

East Coast champion for 1987,
Calvin Fish, shown here at Road America

< 53 >

East Coast champion Steve Shelton

The starting grid for Atlantic's very first oval race at the Milkwaukee Mile - 1988

< 55 >

Undeterred, Hall, Shelton and Swift all bounced back in '88 to claim the titles they missed out on in '87. With Mike Hartgraves and Jerry Marinoff preparing his uniquely liveried Ski Optics DB4, ex-speed skier Hall won five races on his way to the WCAR title, while Shelton took three wins with his Stuart Moore Racing DB4 to collect the HFC crown. Atlantic broadened its appeal as a training category with the first oval race in series history at Milwaukee, where Jocko Cunningham prevailed, and O'Connell closed out the Ralt RT-4's log of success, taking its final win with a dogged performance in the streets of Spokane.

Of those post-Andretti champions, Goodyear went on to win a pair of Michigan 500s, and is now an IRL front runner, while Wood, Prappas and Hall all had brief careers in Indy cars. O'Connell won both the 24-hour sports car race at Daytona and the 12-hour contest at Sebring as part of Nissan's factory team, has raced in the IRL and remains active today.

West Coast champion Dean Hall takes the lead at Riverside, CA - 1988

Road Atlanta - 1988

< 55 >

## The Third Era Dawns

Perhaps the single most important development in the history of the Atlantic formula came in 1989, with the commitment to use Toyota's 1600cc, twin-cam four-cylinder 4A-GE engine as the series' designated power plant. The protracted negotiations toward that end involved a number of people — Toyota's National Motorsports Manager, Les Unger, Bob Anderson and Jon Norman from the SCCA, ECAR boss Vicki O'Connor, Paul Cava and Tim Fortner, who were then administering the WCAR series, and Toyota Racing Development executive VP Masa Suzuki — but ultimately yielded the desired result.

Without Toyota's support, Atlantic could not have achieved what it has, as acknowledged by O'Connor at the time. "In today's world," she said, "you can hardly get track time on a race weekend without a manufacturer behind you. Atlantic wouldn't have been healthy had we stayed the way we were. We had to look at the future." Coincidentally, Yokohama became the official tire supplier for the renamed Toyota Atlantic Championship Brought To You In Part By Yokohama that year and, like Toyota, serves in that capacity today. Toyota's involvement also meant the series would be reunified as a single championship in 1991, but for 1989 and '90 the renamed Atlantic and Pacific divisions continued as separate series. A young Japanese driver named Hiro Matsushita swept to the '89 Pacific crown in Dwayne Anderson's Panasonic Swift, while Jocko Cunningham drove a Steve Dreizler-prepared Swift to the Atlantic title, out-pointing Colin Trueman and closing the year with Cosworth's final Atlantic win. Another footnote was written by '80-'81 champ Jacques Villeneuve's winning drive in a cameo appearance with Pierre Phillips' Swift at Trois-Rivières. Matsushita went on to become the first Japanese driver to race in both the PPG CART World Series and the Indy 500, and currently is part of Toyota's factory effort in the CART series. In 1991 he purchased Swift Cars and began its transformation into Swift Engineering. The company is embarking on its second season of CART racing, and introduces its next generation Atlantic chassis – the 008.a – this year as well.

Steve Shelton's Reynard 89-H at Long Beach, CA - 1989

Pacific division champ Hiro Matsushita is congratulated by Toyota's Les Unger

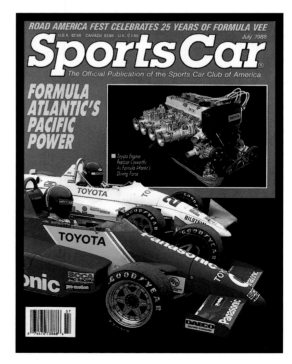

Atlantic champion Jocko Cunningham - 1989

Hiro Matsushita at Long Beach - 1989

Steve Shelton hangs it out a bit too far at Long Beach - 1989

< 57 >

Toyota Grand Prix of Long Beach, CA - 1990

Mark Dismore, who'd scored the first Atlantic win for a Toyota engine at Willow Springs in '89, romped to the 1990 Pacific division championship with Bill Fickling's P1 Swift, and ultimately would record 15 Atlantic wins to eclipse the career record of both Gilles Villeneuve and Claude Bourbonnais. In the East, series rookie Brian Till drove Bob Liebert's Steve Cole-prepared Swift to a trio of victories, as Swift's domination of the formula was challenged by British constructor Reynard. Claude Bourbonnais matched Till's win total with a Reynard, but fell short in the points. Till contested several seasons with CART, but never managed to emulate his Atlantic success.

The twin-series era did create five exceptional race weekends where all the teams from both coasts converged at a single track to do battle. These combined races were run at Memphis in '87, Long Beach in '89 and '90, Heartland Park Topeka in '89 and Road America in '90, and won, chronologically, by R.K. Smith, Hiro Matsushita, Claude Bourbonnais, Mark Dismore and Jimmy Vasser.

Brian Till earned 1990's Atlantic division championship

1990 Pacific division champion Mark Dismore

< 59 >

The reunified series of '91 generated very much a tortoise-and-hare scenario, with Vasser taking his Genoa Racing Swift to six wins and eight poles from the schedule's 13 races, yet losing the championship by four points to Jovy Marcelo, who won twice but used the ever-popular consistency to become Atlantic's first Filipino champion aboard Dwayne Anderson's Swift.

Applying the lessons of his Atlantic experience, Vasser soon moved into CART and proceeded to win both the inaugural U.S. 500 and the PPG Cup championship in 1996. Marcelo, sadly, was killed in a crash during pre-race testing at Indianapolis in 1992.

Jovy Marcello edges ahead of Jimmy Vasser
at Laguna Seca, CA - 1991

< 63 >

The 1992 Toyota Atlantic Championship produced one of the most competitive seasons in series history, with 14 different drivers setting fastest race laps in the year's 14 races. Seven of those also managed to win a race, but from all that parity, Christopher Smith – son of famed crew chief and author Carroll – emerged as series champion in a Swift run by Willi Oppliger and Walt Preston, edging Kiwi Steve Cameron by just five points for the title. The year was also notable for the three wins scored by Mark Dismore, who returned from the broken neck and shattered legs he suffered in a crash during testing at Indianapolis in '91; the four wins and three poles taken by Reynard-mounted drivers (Russell Spence-3 & Harald Huysman-1); and the first Atlantic victories for Ralt's new RT-40 chassis and future champions David Empringham and Patrick Carpentier.

1992 champion Chris Smith

Tom Dooley at Long Beach, CA - 1992

Steve Cameron takes a
break between rounds

< 63 >

Empringham climbed to the top of the championship the following year, when Player's Tobacco returned as the co-title sponsor, with Toyota, of the entire 15-race series after several seasons of supporting only the Canadian rounds.

Despite winning only once, Empringham employed the metronomic consistency of his Victor Sifton-run, Kevin Baltimore-prepared Canaska Ralt to overcome Team Green's Player's twins – Claude Bourbonnais with seven wins and Gilles' 22-year-old son, Jacques, with five. Barry Green's team and young Villeneuve moved together into PPG Cup racing the following year, ultimately winning the Indianapolis 500 and the PPG Cup in 1995 before Jacques moved on to tackle F1. Last year he became Atlantic's second World Champion. Like Rosberg, he drove a Williams to the title.

Claude Bourbonnais and teammate Jacques Villeneuve fight to lead through turn one at the start... but it's a tie when they both pack it into the tire barrier.

Empringham and Villeneuve go wheel to wheel at Montreal, Quebec - 1993

Toronto, Canada - 1993

< 65 >

David Empringham repeats as 1994 champion

Several technical tweaks were made to the formula for the 1994 season as Toyota's engines were converted from carburetors to electronic fuel injection, Yokohama's tires became radials and Ralt brought out the RT-41. Reigning champion Empringham switched his Canadian Tire/Motomaster backing to the Dave McMillan-prepared Ralt American entry and joined countrymen Bill Brack and the Villeneuve brothers as repeat Atlantic titlists. His margin over Lynx Racing's rookie sensation, Richie Hearn, was a mere two points, however, the closest ever. The year also marked the final win for Swift's DB4 chassis, courtesy of Mark Dismore's stunning triumph on the oval at Nazareth. Dismore today pursues his fortunes in the IRL.

Richie Hearn ran strong throughout 1994

Empringham, Hearn and Trueman share the
spoils at Toronto, Canada - 1995

< 69 >

Hearn returned in '95 to turn the tables on Empringham with a late-season charge that secured the title by just four points. The 24-year-old Californian won only three races with John Della Penna's Food 4 Less Ralt – against Empringham's six--but never finished lower than fifth. Like Green and Villeneuve, Della Penna and Hearn moved into Indy cars, and after running with both CART and the IRL in '96 – winning the IRL finale at Las Vegas – they now race exclusively with CART. Empringham went on to become the only driver ever to win championships in both the Atlantic and Indy Lights categories, taking the latter title in 1996.

Hearn shows the way at Trois-Rivières, Canada - 1995

David Empringham nearly three-peated,
with six victories in '95

Richie Hearn and team owner John Della Penna

< 71 >

Patrick Carpentier swept to the 1996 championship with nine wins from 12 races in a Lynx Racing Ralt run by Steve Cameron's Cameron-McGee squad. He closed his unprecedented season with eight consecutive wins from pole position – leading wire to wire in six straight races during the string – to erase the single-season records set by his idol, Gilles Villeneuve, for consecutive victories and consecutive victories from pole position, while matching the ones for wins and wins from pole position.

"You cannot replace somebody like Villeneuve," Carpentier observed at the time, "he is a legend, but I'm very happy about all the records. Maybe I'll be able to say that Gilles Villeneuve helped me in my career because, as I broke so many records, I got a lot of publicity in Canada – and the States, too. It was a big help."

Capitalizing on the experience gained from the champion's test drive program, Carpentier earned a seat with Bettenhausen Racing in CART's PPG Cup series for '97, where he bagged Rookie of the Year honors. For '98 he's teamed with fellow Canadian Greg Moore in a two-car Player's-backed Forsythe Racing effort.

Case Montgomery, Mid-Ohio – 1996

Patrick Carpentier dominated 1996

Chuck West, Patrick Carpentier and Lee
Bentham celebrate a good day's work

Lynx Racing team owner
and number one fan - Peggy Haas

Paul Jasper at Mid-Ohio - 1996

< 73 >

< 75 >

As KOOL Cigarettes assumed co-title sponsorship of the series with Toyota, the 1997 season proved to be an encore for Lynx Racing, except that this time its two rookie drivers won seven races rather than one experienced hand winning nine. Californian Alex Barron overcame a slow start to claim the championship with five victories, while teammate Memo Gidley won twice and kept the title chase mathematically open into its final round. Shortly after the season ended, Barron was selected by Dan Gurney to replace the retiring Juan Fangio ll as PJ Jones' partner in All American Racers' Toyota-powered effort in CART's FedEx Championship Series, the latest Atlantic grad to make it into the major leagues.

Heading into 1998, then, we celebrate the achievements of the past 25 years, while honoring the accomplishments of Atlantic's extended family. The problem with writing the history of this popular formula, however, is that some readers may consider it far too detailed, while others will think it horribly incomplete. Nevertheless, we have tried to provide some insight into the heart and soul of a community that has produced consistently good racing over the years. To any and all who have played a part in that history – and you know who you are – there are only heartfelt thanks and congratulations. May the story never end.

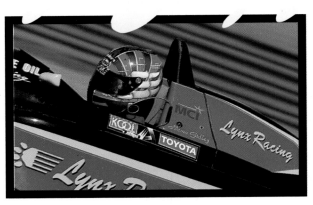

Memo Gidley ran strong for a strong team -
Peggy Haas' Lynx Racing

Alex Barron improved all year to take the '97 title

< 77 >

Foreword
        Atlantic's Number One Son
Introduction
        Vicki O'Connor
        Gerald R. Forsythe
A Quarter Century
        In the Beginning
        Brother Jacques' Turn
        Tires: The Essential Ingredient
        Salvaging the Series
        The Third Era Dawns
Gordon Kirby
Vicki O'Connor
Oh Canada
        Grand Prix of Montreal
        Grand Prix of Trois Rivières
Looking Back
1997 Championship
        Introduction
        The Teams
        The Drivers
        Nowhere without the Teams
        1997 Season's Review
        1997 Final Standings
        1997 KOOL Toyota Awards
Looking Ahead
        One Make for the Future
        Vicki O'Connor

< 81 >

## Gilles Villeneuve

Lionized around the globe as the quintessential racer, Gilles made his name in Atlantic cars between 1974 and 1977, winning championships in '76 and '77. He made the leap to F1 with McLaren before joining Ferrari, where he spun a legendary story as one of Enzo Ferrari's most prized and loved drivers. He was killed in qualifying for the Belgian GP in May, 1982.

## Keke Rosberg

World Champion with the Williams team in 1982, Rosberg won five Grands Prix during a nine-year F1 career that ended with his retirement following the 1986 season. Rosberg also made the leap to F1 from Atlantic, after competing head-to-head with Villeneuve in some of the most classic duels in the formula's history. He also raced successfully in the old Can-Am series, and is now a high-powered agent, handling F1 stars Mika Hakkinen and JJ Lehto.

## Bobby Rahal

A three-time CART champion, and the only man to win the CART championship as an owner/driver. Rahal has won 26 Indy car races, including the Indy 500 in 1986—the first year he won the CART title. An Atlantic graduate from those great days of the mid-'70s, when he raced wheel-to-wheel with Villeneuve and Rosberg. Likely to retire from driving at the end of 1998 when he'll be 45, Rahal will continue as a major CART team owner.

## Michael Andretti

CART's most successful active driver with 36 wins, Andretti won the 1991 CART championship and has been the championship runner-up no fewer than five times – 1986, '87, '90, '92 and '96. His Atlantic title came in 1983 at 20 years of age, and he made his first Indy car start in the fall of that year. Still going strong at 35, he ranks fourth on the all-time winners list behind A.J. Foyt, father Mario and Al Unser Sr.

## Jacques Villeneuve

The 1997 World Champion, 1995 CART champion and Indy 500 winner raced in Toyota Atlantic at the end of 1992 and during all of '93. Villeneuve won five races and finished third in the '93 Toyota Atlantic series before moving on to Indy cars for two years. The 26-year-old son of Gilles scored his first CART win at Elkhart Lake in August of '94, and added four more victories, including the Indy 500, on his way to the '95 CART championship, then moved to F1 with the Williams team.

### Danny Sullivan

The 1988 CART champion and 1985 Indy 500 winner, won 17 Indy car races during a CART career spanning 15 years from 1982-'96. Sullivan started racing in FF1600 in England in 1972, raced F3 in Europe 1973-'75, and F2 in '76. He raced in the North American Atlantic championship in '78 and '80, the Can-Am series for three years, and F1 with Tyrrell in 1983 before moving full-time into Indy cars in 1984. He's now a commentator on ABC TV's coverage of Champ car racing.

### Tom Gloy

A race and championship-winning SCCA Trans-Am team owner who made his reputation in Atlantic cars in the late '70s through 1980. Gloy won Atlantic title in 1979, and was runner-up in '80. He briefly raced Indy cars and then Trans-Am cars, where he was very successful, winning the 1984 championship before establishing one of the category's top teams. His team has moved into NASCAR's Craftsman Truck series for 1998.

### Jimmy Vasser

The 1996 CART champion and U.S. 500 winner, Vasser raced Atlantic cars in 1987, '90 and '91, winning six races and finishing second in the championship in the latter year before breaking into Indy cars in 1992. He started racing in quarter midgets, becoming a three-time national champion before graduating to FF1600s, where he won the West Coast Pro series in '84 and the SCCA National Championshiop in '86.

### Roberto Moreno

The Brazilian fought hard with Michael Andretti for '83 Atlantic title, and has raced F1 and Indy cars with some success over the past 10 years. He finished second in the 1990 Japanese GP for the Benetton team, and performed impressively well as a stand in for the injured Christian Fittipaldi in six CART races with Newman/Haas during '97. Also drove Mercedes GT car in '97. Came up through carts, FF1600 and F3 before Atlantic.

### Bob Earl & Brian Robertson

Earl raced Atlantic cars in the late '70s and early '80s. He went on to win IMSA GTP races with the factory Nissan team, and is one of the most respected race-driving instructors and coaches in the country. Robertson won the Player's Challenge championship for Formula B in 1972, and as the North American importer for Ralt Cars ran one of the most successful Atlantic teams for many years. A big contributor to the success of the formula over the years.

*Gordon Kirby celebrated his 25th season as Autosport's American Editor in 1997, specializing in CART championship car racing, but has watched and covered many Toyota Atlantic races over the years. In fact, the first race he covered for Autosport was an SCCA Formula B—the precursor to Formula Atlantic—championship round at Mosport in 1968.*

< 83 >

—Vicki O'Connor

Foreword
    Atlantic's Number One Son
Introduction
    Vicki O'Connor
    Gerald R. Forsythe
A Quarter Century
    In the Beginning
    Brother Jacques' Turn
    Tires: The Essential Ingredient
    Salvaging the Series
    The Third Era Dawns
Gordon Kirby
Vicki O'Connor
Oh Canada
    Grand Prix of Montreal
    Grand Prix of Trois Rivières
Looking Back
1997 Championship
    Introduction
    The Teams
    The Drivers
    Nowhere without the Teams
    1997 Season's Review
    1997 Final Standings
    1997 KOOL Toyota Awards
Looking Ahead
    One Make for the Future
    Vicki O'Connor

< 85 >

## Vicki O'Connor
## From racer's wife to series president:

Vicki O'Connor first discovered racing when she met her future husband, Bill, on a blind date. Vicki was working as an administrative assistant to the chairman of the board of a Chicago-based advertising firm, while Bill, who owned a commercial art studio, spent his free time working on a friend's E-Production Porsche Speedster.

"He wanted to race himself, that was his goal. I thought that was great. I said, `Why not, go for it,'" explains O'Connor. "He started racing a month after we were married, in 1968. We took every last penny we had and got a loan and went racing. I thought it was exciting. I knew nothing about it. It was something no one that I knew had done. I just thought, `Boy, is this great!'"

When the Player's Challenge Atlantic series was formed out of the Formula B national championship in Canada in 1974, Bill O'Connor was there, campaigning a Lola 360 for importer Carl Haas with much success. Vicki was there, too, booking hotel reservations for the crew, ordering food, doing the timing and scoring – even polishing wheels.

"Bill did very well in tough fields, with drivers like Villeneuve, Rahal, and names you may not even know who were faster than they were," O'Connor says. "He still had his business and I still worked. We'd leave work on Thursday, hook the trailer up to the van and drive all night across the 401, to places like Gimli, Manitoba, Trois-Rivières, Sanair, Tremblant. If it were a far-away place like Halifax, we'd leave on an early flight Monday morning to be back at work."

O'Connor's day job was working as a secretary for Haas. While the wild lifestyle of a racer's wife taught her the hands-on aspects of the sport, it was under Haas' tutelage that she learned the more practical, business side of racing to complete what she calls her Ph.D. in Motorsports.

"I learned how a business runs – everything from accounts payable, accounts receivable, parts ordering, invoicing, customer letters. It was just good business practice, and I was able to have a hand in a lot of that. Also, because it was racing related, I met a lot of people in the industry, which probably helped when I went out on my own. People knew me."

In the early 1980s, a group of Midwest racers took an interest in Sports 2000 cars, and decided to form a pro series. They asked for O'Connor's help registering drivers and organizing race dates. It was the beginning of a remarkable career as a series president, and sent O'Connor on the road to reviving and nurturing the Atlantic series, which had hit troubled times.

"I ran Sports 2000 out of my house. My next door neighbor, Joyce Saifuku, who is still my secretary, managed the office during the day and then I worked on it at night and weekends. I still had a full-time job at Carl Haas Auto," she says.

"I did all the paperwork for a race at Mid-Ohio. Then I thought, well, this was sort of fun, so I called the then president of Road America, who I knew pretty well, and I said, 'Well, you're always looking for support races. How about if we help this group?' We created the Road America Cup, which raced every pro weekend. One year we had 52 cars take the green flag."

Sports 2000 eventually grew and became the Oldsmobile Pro Series. O'Connor's work there established a reputation for her company, Pro-Motion Agency, Ltd. So it was only natural when, in 1985, a similar group of fledgling Atlantic drivers asked for her help once again.

"Holly Angus, whose husband, Mike, was racing Atlantic and was one of the early champions of the series, was the first to start ECAR, for East Coast Atlantic Racing," O'Connor says. "It was modeled on the WCAR series that had started on the West Coast. She asked me to see what I could do with it. The SCCA thought it was a good idea and agreed to sanction it."

"It took me a long time to decide to do it. I loved Atlantic, but Sports 2000 was very successful at the time and Atlantic was very dilapidated. I didn't know if I had what it took to get it where it needed to go in what I saw as a changing motorsports landscape. It was a complete resuscitation. There was a lot of building to do. It needed to get more serious if it was going to reach a certain level. Dates became more and more difficult to get because there were more series. It needed more professionalism; it needed sponsorship. I thought, what if I failed?"

Far from failing, under O'Connor's leadership the Atlantic series blossomed into one of the most successful feeder series in North American motorsports, with solid financial backing from co-title sponsors Toyota and KOOL, plus the series' original sponsor, Player's, as well as from long-time sponsors TRD USA Inc. and the Yokohama Tire Corporation.

"Perhaps one of the reasons I was able to succeed with the series is because I understood Atlantic, believed in the series, and thought like the drivers and teams," O'Connor says. "Initially, it was a difficult group to manage, and many times I have referred to ourselves as outlaws. We have a different mind set. We like racing a certain way. We like cars a certain way. I adored the people, the travel, the competition, the excitement – every bit of it. I guess you could say it's who I am."

< 87 >

## Oh Canada

Foreword
        Atlantic's Number One Son
Introduction
        Vicki O'Connor
        Gerald R. Forsythe
A Quarter Century
        In the Beginning
        Brother Jacques' Turn
        Tires: The Essential Ingredient
        Salvaging the Series
        The Third Era Dawns
Gordon Kirby
Vicki O'Connor
Oh Canada
        Grand Prix of Montreal
        Grand Prix of Trois Rivières
Looking Back
1997 Championship
        Introduction
        The Teams
        The Drivers
        Nowhere without the Teams
        1997 Season's Review
        1997 Final Standings
        1997 KOOL Toyota Awards
Looking Ahead
        One Make for the Future
        Vicki O'Connor

< 89 >

## AFTER 25 YEARS, THE ATLANTIC NOW COVERS NORTH AMERICA.

As one of its earliest sponsors, Player's Ltd. is proud to have helped the Atlantic Series grow to a championship whose 12 races take place from coast to coast across North America. And whose fierce competition has fostered the development of some of the greatest names in open-wheel racing. We look forward to continuing our association with Atlantic racing as sponsor of the four Player's Challenge races in Canada.

### CONGRATULATIONS!

The Atlantic series grew from the seed of the Formula B national championship that was planted in Canada during the late '60s and early '70s. Though the series has grown tremendously since that time and has become an important element of motor racing throughout North America, race fans in Canada have continued to maintain a close relationship with Atlantic. Today the series races in Vancouver, Toronto, Trois-Rivières and Montreal, and Player's, the original sponsor, offers a separate prize fund for those events. All four races draw the biggest crowds on the circuit. At Vancouver and Toronto, the Atlantic cars run in support of the CART FedEx Championship Series, like they do in much of the season. But the races at Montreal and Trois-Rivières have always had a special stature.

## Grand Prix of Montreal

Once a year, the tranquillity of a waterfront park gives way to the scream of race engines. Visitors to the Grand Prix of Montreal are greeted by a sea of fleur-de-lis flags waving in the crowd, and by a torrent of French rolling off the tongues of the locals. To attend the Grand Prix is to immerse yourself in a unique world of Gallic culture blended with cosmopolitan flair. Located on a subway line within easy reach of downtown Montreal, the race at the Circuit Gilles Villeneuve regularly attracts more than 100,000 revelers. Much more than a simple race, the Grand Prix is the climax of a full week of parades, parties and other festivities downtown. Give the Quebecois a reason to show off their fierce, European-like passion for racing, and you have an electric atmosphere.

The words ``Salut, Gilles,'' painted on the start/finish line alert drivers that this is not a typical race. Gilles Villeneuve, of course, parlayed astounding success in Atlantic into a seat with Ferrari in Formula One. He also won his first-ever grand prix on this circuit. His legacy weighs heavily over this event. While Atlantic drivers race before the Champ car community year round, only once do they get the opportunity to showcase their talents to the Grand Prix world where Villeneuve made his mark. It is an opportunity they savor.

Classic battles at a diverse array of Canadian circuits, including St. Jovite...

...and Westwood laid the groundwork for today's Atlantic events

< 91 >

The 2.74-mile Circuit Gilles Villeneuve was built in 1978 and has hosted the Canadian Grand Prix ever since. The only other temporary circuit with such an exclusive and long-standing relationship with F1 is Monaco. The circuit is located on the Ile Notre Dame, a man-made island that was constructed as the site of Expo '67, the world's fair hosted in Montreal during Canada's centennial year.

As the Circuit Gilles Villeneuve has become a mainstay of the F1 calendar, so too has the Grand Prix weekend become a permanent highlight of the Atlantic schedule. Atlantic cars first raced in Montreal in 1978, and have since become an integral part of the weekend. The Saturday Atlantic race never fails to pack the stands.

Imagine, then, the rapture that overcame Bertrand Godin, a Quebecer from nearby St. Hyacinthe, when, driving for the Player's-backed Forsythe Racing team, he won his first ever Atlantic event at this sacred venue. "This is a dream come true," said the 29-year-old veteran of French FF1600 and Indy Lights, overcome by emotion. "It's wonderful to win in front of our home crowd, in front of the Player's people."

## Grand Prix of Trois-Rivières

Godin's teammate, Alexandre Tagliani, had a similar triumph when he won the Atlantic round at the Grand Prix of Trois-Rivières, Canada's classic motorsports event. Like the Ile Notre-Dame in Montreal on which the Circuit Gilles-Villeneuve was built, the Grand Prix de Trois-Rivières was first conceived as part of Canada's centennial celebrations in 1967. It is North America's oldest street circuit, and the Duplessis Gate under which the cars pass has become one of the most famous and enduring images in Canadian motor racing.

In its early years the event featured as headliners Formula B – the national Canadian championship that preceded Atlantic, as well as production-based sports cars and Formula 5000. Atlantic was formed in 1974 and debuted at Trois-Rivières that same year. The series and the event grew up together, and the popularity of Atlantic was instrumental in reviving the Trois-Rivières race in 1989, the same year that Toyota signed on as the major series sponsor.

Chip Mead, Damien Magee and Tom Klausler locked
in battle at Trois Rivières - 1975

If Trois-Rivières has a claim to fame, it is the pop legend created by Gilles Villeneuve there in 1976. A former snowmobile racer and Formula Ford driver, Villeneuve stunned the world by defeating an impressive list of Formula One pilots who had been invited to compete in a special 10th anniversary running of the race. They included Vittorio Brambilla, Patrick Depailler, Patrick Tambay, future F1 champion Alan Jones, and James Hunt, who would go on to win the F1 title that year.

Ever since, glory at Trois-Rivières has been the goal of every Canadian driver, and the race has blossomed into one of Canada's most important sporting events.

"Not only do you have very enthusiastic race fans at Trois-Rivières and Montreal, which is wonderful for us, but you are also in the beautiful province of Quebec," says series president Vicki O'Connor. "Both races are favorite events for everyone in series."

Bertrand Godin and Alexandre Tagliani at Trois-Rivières - 1997

< 93 >

Foreword
    Atlantic's Number One Son
Introduction
    Vicki O'Connor
    Gerald R. Forsythe
A Quarter Century
    In the Beginning
    Brother Jacques' Turn
    Tires: The Essential Ingredient
    Salvaging the series
    The Third Era Dawns
Gordon Kirby
Vicki O'Connor
Oh Canada
    Grand Prix of Montreal
    Grand Prix of Trois Rivières
Looking Back
1997 Championship
    Introduction
    The Teams
    The Drivers
    Nowhere without the Teams
    1997 Season's Review
    1997 Final Standings
    1997 KOOL Toyota Awards
Looking Ahead
    One Make for the Future
    Vicki O'Connor

< 95 >

### Jimmy Vasser:

I dig Atlantic. When I got my chance to drive an Atlantic car for the first time, I was scared of it. It was this big race car. But it was just a kick in the pants to drive. It had tons of grip, tons of downforce, and a good power-to-weight ratio. It's just incredible.

One of my first races I won was at Laguna Seca race in 1987. It was in front of the Indy car crowd. That was my first big professional victory.

In 1990 John Della Penna called me and asked me to drive his car. It was a Sears Point race on Sunday and I think he called me on Saturday. So I started in the back and I was up to like third or fourth after a few laps in. I only did a few races that year. That was when they had East coast and West coast series, and they had a big East/West shoot-out. I sat on pole and won that one.

Then Rick Galles decided he would put his son with our team, so in '91 we did a two-car Atlantic team with Jamie Galles and it all kind of snowballed. I think I won like seven races that year. I won every race I finished, but Jovy Marcello beat me by a few points. Even though I didn't win the championship, I think people noticed. I met Jim Hayoe and Rick Cole through the Atlantic series. They formed an Indy car team in '92 that was my start. Atlantic was the class that always gave me my showcase in front of all the Indy car guys and all the decision makers. Being able to show my talent in front of all those guys was just everything for me.

### Michael Andretti:

I think the Atlantic series was a very important step in my career. The cars were more technically advanced. You could do more with them and they reacted more like real race cars. I was with a great team with Brian Robertson. He really understood those cars. We were trying all kinds of different things, which I was never used to before. It was a good experience for me. We were constantly trying to develop the car. I think that was the year I learned a lot about setting a race car up, which helped me a lot in Indy cars.

I raced in Atlantic in 1983, and I did the last three Indy car races that year. So I stepped right from Atlantics to Indy car. It was a good stepping stone. The exposure you got in it was good and the competition was tough. That year my main competition was Roberto Moreno. We had some great races together.

### Bobby Rahal:

I was fortunate enough to be a part of what was really a renaissance period in the Atlantic championship. When you consider that you were racing against the likes of Keke Rosberg and Gilles Villeneuve, it really gives you an idea of the quality of competition that existed in the series at that time and reinforces the sense of real accomplishment that came with winning races. That experience and the competition were vital to the next steps I eventually took in racing.

### Scott Goodyear:

I was in Atlantic in 1986, driving for Tom Mitchell out of Houston, Texas. There were nine races, and we won five of them, had five poles and five fastest laps. That's what started getting me noticed by Indy car teams. It was the Ralt RT-4 chassis in '86, which was still an aluminum monocoque tub. When I went back in 1989 to do two races, it was the Swift chassis. Those were sort of like mini Indy cars, which is what they are now.

A lot of rising stars have been through Atlantic. As a driver progresses through the racing ranks, if you can be successful in Formula Atlantic, you know you'll be competitive in Indy cars.

### Richie Hearn:

I really enjoyed Atlantics. Racing seemed so simple then. The higher up you go, the driving is less and the business is more.

The cars are great to drive – much more fun than Indy cars. The Indy car is fun, but it's heavy. In Atlantic, the power and weight is very manageable. You can do a lot of things without getting in trouble. Also, the standing start is one of the most exciting things in motorsports. I miss that.

Atlantic cars are much closer to Indy cars than anything else we have in North America. A lot of that is because of the tunnels and the fact that you're allowed to engineer the cars anyway you like. We did a lot with shock technology. We did a lot with rear suspension geometry. You really learn what you want in a race car.

The Atlantic series was my first real, professional series. It has a high level of exposure. A lot of Indy car teams watch the Atlantic races. It also has a lot of history that carries over and you feel it when you're doing well. For me, it was a big deal to race at Long Beach. That was a race I'd been going to for so long, but always on the other side of the fence.

### Patrick Carpentier:

Driving in Atlantic was a very good learning curve for me, especially with the team I was with, Lynx Racing. They were very well organized, they could perform very well, and I learned what it was like to be with a winning team.

It helped me a lot on the mechanical side, and you go to a lot of the same tracks as the CART series. It was a good stepping stone. When I first tested an Indy car with Arciero-Wells it went really well because it was just like driving the Atlantic car, just faster, so I got used to that very quickly. And then I had my test with Bettenhausen, and that went really well also.

I remember when I was young Stephane Proulx was racing Atlantic. He was always my hero. Also Jacques Villeneuve the uncle was in Atlantic. I remember going to the Canadian Grand Prix with my father and dreaming of that series. I remember I was looking at the cars and I asked a mechanic what that spoon was – it was a sway bar fork in the back, and I called it a spoon. That was the first thing about a race car that I learned. He tried to explain it to me and I didn't have a clue. It's funny how life is. When you're young you look at it and it's like something untouchable, and then one day you're in it, and then one day you pass through it, and then you make it to CART. It's a dream come true.

### Roberto Moreno:

Atlantic has really been my most successful formula. I won the FIA World Cup, the New Zealand championship, three Australian Grands Prix, the New Zealand Grand Prix, and I finished second in the North American championship in 1983 to Michael Andretti.

Two weeks before the '83 season started, I lost my sponsor. We showed up at Willow Springs with the car on a rented open trailer, and me and the mechanics and our girlfriends all in the cab together. We had all of our spare parts tie-wrapped to the car, so you couldn't even tell it was a race car. We parked next to this enormous black rig – it was Michael Andretti's. You should have seen the look on his mechanics' faces when we pulled up.

That year if I won a race I received $5000 in prize money, and we used that to race the following weekend. I won four races, but Michael finished second in all of them. He won three races, and I either didn't start or didn't finish those, so he won the championship. Atlantic was very important because it helped me learn more F1 circuits than any other beginning F1 driver. When I got to F1, I already knew Long Beach and Detroit and Montreal. Also, the horsepower and the grip **were** closer to an F1 car than to an F3 car.

It also was well-recognized in **America**, and I wanted to race here in the future.

< 97 >

© 1998 B&WT Co

SURGEON GENERAL'S WARNING: Quitting Smoking Now Greatly Reduces Serious Risks to Your Health.

B
KOOL

Foreword
    Atlanta's Number One Son
Introduction
    Vicki O'Connor
    Gerald R. Forsythe
A Quarter Century
    It's a Beginning
    Brother Jacques' Turn
    Time: The Essential Ingredient
    Salvaging the Series
    The Third Era Dawns
Gordon Kirby
Vicki O'Connor
Oh Canada
    Grand Prix of Montreal
    Grand Prix of Trois Rivieres
Looking Back
1997 Championship
    Introduction
    The Teams
    The Drivers
    Nowhere without the Fans
    1997 Seasons Review
    1997 Final Standings
    PPG KOOL Toyota Awards
Looking Ahead
    One Make for the future
    Vicki O'Connor

< 101 >

Dear Readers:

In 1989, when Toyota began its involvement with the Atlantic series as co-sponsor and official engine supplier, we viewed our participation as a marketing opportunity to show-case Toyota technology. Then, as now, using Toyota Racing Development exclusively for all engine-related research and design, Toyota is committed to providing the necessary tools to enhance the future generation of open-wheel race car drivers.

While the past nine years have seen three major evolutions in chassis design, the Toyota 4A-GE engine has changed little. The most significant change came in 1994 when TRD updated the powerplant from carburetion to fuel injection. Throughout its career, the 4A-GE engine has set a standard for performance, reliability and longevity that few race engines can equal today.

With the introduction of the new Swift chassis, 1998 will also see an upgraded TRD engine management system that will simulate those used in Indy cars. The new system features fully sequential injection as well as the capability to run ``shift-with-out-lift'' in the cars.

Technology continues to march relentlessly forward, but without a simple and effective training ground for new drivers, we will have no heroes to showcase that technology. As the likes of Bobby Rahal, Michael Andretti, Jimmy Vasser, Jacques Villeneuve, Richie Hearn, Patrick Carpentier and most recently, Alex Barron have shown, the Atlantic formula works.

The Atlantic championship works because our sponsor partners, KOOL, Player's and Yokohama Tire, also believe that providing a competitive and professional training ground is necessary for the future of open-wheel racing. We are thrilled to have such dynamic and aggressive partners to share in the marketing and promotion of Atlantic into the next millennium.

To close, Toyota would like to thank Vicki O'Connor and her staff at Pro-Motion Agency, Ltd. for their tireless dedication and unequaled level of professionalism in administering the series. To each of the Atlantic teams, we wish you the best of luck for a safe and competitive 25th Anniversary Season.

Sincerely,

Les Unger
National Motorsports Manager
Toyota Motors Sales, U.S.A., Inc.

< 103 >

This is our

Lambeau Field.

Our Boston Garden.

Our Camden Yard.

We play

on asphalt

and concrete.

Grass is for

the infield.

No matter

the sport,

we're all

athletes.

But out here,

when things get rough,

you can't call a time-out.

TOYOTA
motor sports

PPG/CART World Series racing. Where athletes move at speeds up to 240 mph. Witness the Toyota-powered MCI and Castrol/Jockey cars and you'll soon understand why Indy car racing is one of the fastest sports in the world. Toyota Motorsports. Our minds are always racing.

www.toyota.com

©1997 Toyota Motor Sales, U.S.A., Inc.

## LYNX RACING - 1997 OVERVIEW

Lynx Racing, owned by Peggy Haas and Jackie Doty, is one of the most unique and successful 'driver development' organizations in auto racing today. The team's purpose is to seek out drivers with the capability to become champions, provide them with the training and resources to achieve their potential, and help them make the jump to the top levels of auto racing. Lynx Racing driver Patrick Carpentier won the 1996 KOOL/Toyota Atlantic Championship with victories in 9 of 12 races – eight of them in a row from the pole – and went on to win the 1997 CART 'Rookie of the Year' award driving for Bettenhausen/Alumax.

In 1997, Lynx Racing competed in three different open-wheel racing series – the KOOL/Toyota Atlantic Championship, U.S. Formula 2000 Championship and Star Formula Mazda Championship – with four drivers (Alex Barron, Memo Gidley, Buddy Rice and Sara Senske). Each of them demonstrated beyond question that they have the "right stuff" to become auto racing's stars of the future.

While Lynx Racing's F2000 and Formula Mazda 'junior teams' are in their first season, the Atlantic team has finished in the top five for the last five years in a row. This includes two 'Rookie of the Year' awards (Richie Hearn in 1994 and Alex Barron in 1997) and two championships (Patrick Carpentier in 1996 and Alex Barron in 1997). In the past three years, Lynx Racing has scored 18 wins and 16 poles in 36 Toyota Atlantic races, an eloquent testimonial to the team's training program which focuses equally on driving/technical skills and personal/spiritual development.

## KOOL/Toyota Atlantic Championship

For the second year in a row, Lynx Racing – under the guidance of team manager/driving coach Steve Cameron, crew chief Rick Cameron and engineer Jim Griffith – dominated the fiercely competitive KOOL/Toyota Atlantic Championship. The team's back-to-back championships were both won during qualifying with a pole position performance – Carpentier at Road America in 1996 and Barron at Laguna Seca in 1997.

Alex Barron, 27, of Vista, California, won the hard-fought Atlantic championship in his rookie season – only his second year of racing cars after an international, multi-championship career in karting. With the support of friend and mentor Billy Ewing and Victory Circle Racing, Barron had the sort of season only a true 'phenom' can produce: five wins (Nazareth, Milwaukee, Mid-Ohio, Road America, Laguna Seca), four poles (Nazareth, Milwaukee, Toronto, Laguna Seca), seven 'fastest race laps', nine podium finishes, 'Rookie of the Year' and the series' championship.

Barron's 1997 Lynx Racing teammate, Memo Gidley, 27, of San Rafael, California, was also an Atlantic rookie. He won the prestigious and hotly-contested 'Player's Challenge' championship-within-a-championship which is awarded to the driver scoring the most points in the four Canadian rounds (Montreal - 3rd, Toronto - 1st, Trois-Rivières - 5th, Vancouver - 1st + pole) of the series. He also finished second in the series championship, won two races, scored one pole and five podium finishes.

< 105 >

Gidley impressed a variety of people, both long-time personal sponsors and CART team owners, with a series of forceful drives beginning with a front-row starting spot and second-place finish at the season's first race in Homestead. In the off season, Gidley tested with several Indy Lights teams, and won the GT America Stock Car class at the Reno Grand Prix.

In addition to driver honors, Lynx Racing's pit crews (Jason Robb/Tom Darms for Gidley and Mike West/Satoshi Mori for Barron), each won one of the two Player's Pit Stop Competitions held during the season, and collectively won the coveted "Masters of the Pit Stop" championship. And Lynx Racing's engine supplier, Paul Hasselgren, expanded on his astounding record of two championship seasons in a row without a single engine failure, winning the Atlantic series' 'TRD Engine Builder of the Year' award for the second year in a row.

## U.S. F2000 Championship

1997 marked Lynx Racing's first foray into the motorsports whirlwind that is the U.S. F2000 Championship with a car fielded by Lynx Racing/ DSTP Motorsports for Buddy Rice, 21, of Phoenix, Arizona.

DSTP fields one of Lynx Racing's 'junior teams', and, like Lynx, is owned by a woman, Dede Rushton, and run by a woman, Pam Griffith. It also shares with Lynx Racing the management/coaching skills of Steve Cameron and engineering expertise of Jim Griffith. Lynx's KOOL/Toyota Atlantic champions, Alex Barron and Memo Gidley, are both graduates of DSTP Motorsports and the U.S. F2000 series.

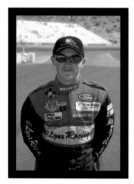

With fields frequently topping 40 cars and the top dozen cars all qualifying within a few tenths of a second of each other, Rice rose to a commanding lead atop the championship points battle twice during the series' 12-race season and established himself indelibly as a rising star. He started on the pole in his first race at Walt Disney World and won the third race, on the Phoenix International Raceway's 1-mile oval. During the course of the 12-race season he sat on the pole twice, qualified in the top 10 ten times and scored five podium finishes. The rest of the season, however, was a constant struggle with mechanical maladies over which he had no control, relegating him to a fourth-place finish in the championship.

In the post season, Rice and fellow U.S. F2000 competitor Matt Sielsky were selected from a group of the best young drivers in America as winners of the eighth annual Valvoline Team USA Scholarship. Lynx Atlantic driver Memo Gidley was also a Valvoline Team USA Scholarship driver in 1995. The Rice/Sielsky duo carried the Team USA colors at the Formula Opel Series Nations Cup VIII event at Donington Park, England, on October 18-19 and scored a combined finish of fifth overall among teams from 22 nations.

## Star Formula Mazda Championship

The newest driver in Lynx Racing's stable of champions-in-the-making is Sara Senske, an 18-year old from Kennewick, Washington. She's from a racing family (her father was the 1989 SCCA production class rally champion), has been competing in karts since she was seven years old, winning her first race at eight.

Senske came to the attention of Lynx Racing in 1996 as a top driver in the Skip Barber Racing School 'Western Series' and signed with the team in 1997. Kent

Stacy and his top-ranked S3 Racing team were recruited to field a Lynx-backed car for her in the final five races of the ultra-competitive Star Formula Mazda Championship.

Formula Mazdas are spec single-seaters powered by Mazda rotary engines, and fields in the West Coast series are frequently even larger than the U.S. FF2000, sometimes starting as many as 50 cars. The series is a cost-effective training ground that also requires the driver to learn the intricacies of suspension setup and interpretation of on-board computer data.

Senske proved a quick study, regularly qualifying and finishing in the top 10. In the final race of the season, a 'bonus' event in support of the IRL season finale at the Las Vegas Motor Speedway, she qualified on the pole in her first-ever oval track race and led the first 20 laps. Deteriorating handling on her car ultimately moved her back to a twelfth-place finish, but it was an impressive effort that argues well for her future in open wheel racing.

## Lynx Racing in 1998

As early as the Milwaukee race, Atlantic driver Alex Barron was having conversations with various CART teams, but he intelligently chose to wait until the end of the season to make any decisions. In his first CART test, with the Arciero-Wells team (part of his prize for winning the Atlantic championship), he so impressed the team with his driving and technical feedback that they immediately offered him a contract for testing and four races in 1998 with a full season in 1999.

Proving that he's not only fast but lucky, the unexpected retirement of CART driver Juan Manuel Fangio II brought Barron a competing full season offer from Dan Gurney's All-American Racers. He quickly signed and will be P.J. Jones' teammate for the 1998 CART FedEx Championship, driving a Toyota-powered Reynard sponsored by Castrol and hoping to be Lynx Racing's second graduate in a row to win the CART Rookie of the Year title.

In the KOOL/Toyota Atlantic Championship, Memo Gidley will return for a second season, partnered by Lynx/DSTP F2000 graduate Buddy Rice. The duo will compete in new Swift 008.a cars with Hasselgren Engines and Yokohama tires. Rice will be competing for the team's third Rookie of the Year award and will run #65. Gidley will run the traditional Lynx Racing #19, the number Carpenter carried in his record-breaking championship season.

In the Star Formula Mazda West Championship, Sara Senske will run a full schedule of 13 races on 11 weekends (two weekends have one race Saturday and another on Sunday). Her #19 Lynx Racing Formula Mazda will again be prepared and fielded by Kent Stacy and S3 Racing. She will be competing for the series championship, with a view toward moving up to the Lynx/DSTP F2000 team in 1999.

In the U.S. F2000 Championship, DSTP Motorsports will field cars for regular drivers Ric Rushton and Tom Wood. In addition, the team will campaign a car, with technical support from Lynx Racing, for Bobby Oergel, a 23 year-old karting champion from Kerman, California who won three of six races in the West Coast F2000 series in 1997.

< 107 >

Binder Racing

**John Binder**
275 Palmer Rd., N.E.
Calgary, Alberta
Canada, T2E 7G4
(403) 250-2644  Fax (403) 250-2622

B.D.J.S., Inc.

**Brian Robertson**
23110 Kashiwa Court
Torrance, CA  90505
(310) 533-1144  Fax (310) 530-0139

BRS Motorsports

**Robert Sollenskog**
P.O. Box 422
Antioch, IL 60002
(847) 395-4244 Fax (847) 295-5811

C B R Enterprises

**Carlos Bobeda**
8414 Corbin Avenue
Northridge, CA  91324
(818) 993-7419  Fax (818) 993-7420

Cameron McGee Motorsports /
Lynx Racing

**Steve Cameron**
29121 Arnold Drive
Sonoma, CA  95476
(707) 996-1112  Fax (707) 996-9148

Competition Preparation

**Dennis Eade**
P.O. Box 97
Zenda, WI  53195
(414) 275-9806  Fax (414) 275-1964

D.L. Racing

**Dave Meehan**
144 Mariner Drive, Unit D
Southampton, NY  19968
(516) 287-7190  Fax  (516) 287-7186

Sandy Dells Racing

**Sandy Dells**
1469 Montgomery Drive
Vista, CA  92084
(760) 758-4510  Fax  (760) 758-8131

Different Drummer Racing

**Greg Sorrentino**
P.O. Box 124
Troy, MI  48099
(810) 775-4488 Fax (810) 608-2588

Intercar Motorsports

**Joe Tabor**
208 Franklin
El Segundo, CA  92045
(310)  322-3008  Fax  (310) 322-3032

Thomas E. Johnston Engineering

**Tom Johnston**
116-930 W. 1st Street
North Vancouver, B.C.
Canada  V7P 3N4
(604) 986-5336 Fax (604) 980-3747

J&J Racing

**Mike Grubb**
103 S. Church Street
Bally, PA  19503
(610) 845-2848  Fax  (610) 845-8820

## Olsson Engineering
**Ove Olsson**
13743 Laurel Drive, Unit C
Lake Forrest, IL 60045
Ph. & Fax (847) 362-7723

## P-1 Racing
**Bill Fickling**
1027 Calle Trepadora, #4
San Clements, CA 92673
(714) 498-7271  Fax  (714) 498-7439

## PDR Enterprises
**Michael David**
1800 Capital Street
Corona, CA 91719
(909) 735-7710  Fax  (909) 737-4982

## Phillips Motorsports
**Pierre Phillips**
P.O. Box 2642
15645 S.E. 114th Avenue, Unit 210
Clackamas, OR 97015
(503) 656-4483

## Player's/Forsythe Racing
**Neil Mickelwright/Kelly Loewen**
7231 Georgetown Road
Indianapolis, IN 46268
(317) 216-9000 Fax (317) 216-9099

## Precision Preperation Inc. (PPI)
**Nick Harvey**
30212 Tomas
Rancho Santa Margarita, CA 92688
(714) 589-5394  Fax (714) 589-5964

## RDS Motorsports, Inc.
**Alfredo Rizza di Sardi**
71 Sovereign Court, Unit 43
Woodbridge, Ontario, Canada  L4L 8S9
(905) 264-4111  Fax  (905) 264-1462

## Michael Shank Racing Services
**Michael Shank**
1386 Fields Avenue
Columbus, OH 43211
(614) 299-3811  Fax  (614) 299-4157

## Weld Motorsports
**Skip Weld**
31024 Quail Hollow
Sorrento, FL 32776
(352) 383-5158  Fax  (352) 383-5438

## World Speed Motorsports
**Chuck West**
29115 Arnold Drive, Unit E-4
Sonoma, CA 95476
(707) 939-8312 Fax (707) 939-0806

< 109 >

Yoichi Akase Frank Allers    Mattias And
Tony Ave    Joao Barbosa    Alex Barro
Cam Binder    Ian Bland Russ Bo
Antoine Bimiyard Bill Auberlen Kelvin Cogan
Mike Conte Stuart Crow    David
Joao Barbosa
Michael David    Joaquin DeS
George Frazier Cam Binder
Brian French    Marcelo Caffoglio
Michael David
Dave Hall    Michael David    Greg Harrington
James Irvin Bertrand Godin    Jansen
Lang    Anthony Lazzaro    Howi
Eric Lang
Peter MacLeod    Bob McGregor Case
Leo Parente Case Montgomery Peters Da
Pugliese    Stephanie Roy    Jo
Ted Sahley    Je
David Rutledge    Ted Sahley
Jeret Schisseder Sollenskog Simpson
Sollenskog    Joe Sposato Carol
Mark Tague    Chuck
Alexandre Tagliani Mark Tague    Bo
Dan Vosloo    Jim Ward
Scott Wood

Dennis Asbury

Bill Auberlen

Brian Battaglia

John Brooks     Buddy Brundo          Mark

Tony Ave

Cutler

Barron

John E. "Nick" Ferguson          Steve Forrer

David Cutler

Memo Gidley          Bertrand Godin

Memo Gidley     Andy Maryonto     Paul Hidalgo

Steve Knapp     Steve Knapp          Eric

Liebengood     Keith Lively

Montgomery     Anthony Lazzaro

Charles Nearburg

Pook     Bill Pratt          Jimmy

Rutherford

Schroeder

Mike Sauce

Alex Siska     Chris Smith     Tagliani     Robert

Sergei Szortyka

Kenny Wilden

Thomas     Bill Tichenor

Chuck West     Kenny Wilden

< 111 >

## Alex Barron,
## Vista Calif.   (R)
06-11-70, San Diego, Calif.

*Alex Barron*

**background**
first year in Atlantic racing following an illustrious
tenure in karting and Formula Ford 2000 — began
his racing career in go-karts at age nine — won
regional, state and national karting titles between
1985 and 1995 — three-time National Champion in
1995 in three different International Karting Federation (I.K.F.)
125cc divisions including 125 Moto, 125 Open, 125 Road

**1996 season**
California State Champion in 125cc Shifter Karts — competed in the
U.S. Pro Formula Ford 2000 Championship, where he finished sev-
enth overall and scored a season-best third place at Las Vegas

**personal**
single — enjoys boxing, mountain biking, and ping pong

## Memo Gidley,
## San Rafael,
## Calif.   (R)
09-29-69, La Paz, Mexico

*Memo Gidley*

**background**
1992 Russell Racing School Champion
(Laguna Seca Raceway) — 1994 U.S. 80cc
Gearbox Kart champion — named "Rookie-of-the-
Year" in 1995 U.S. Formula Ford 2000
Championship, and won the 1995 Oval Course
Championship award — also named a Team USA
Scholarship winner in 1995 — test driver and coach for Trackmagic
Racing Karts

**1996 season**
won the 1996 U.S. 125cc Gearbox Kart (USKA) championship

**personal**
single — enjoys sailing

## Alexandre Tagliani,
## Lachenaie,
## Que.,Canada
10-18-72, Montreal, Que.

**background**
second-year Atlantic driver beginning his first season with the Player's/Forsythe Racing Team — former Canadian karting and ice-skating star —
Quebec 100cc Junior Kart Champion in 1987 at age
15 — won championship in every other Kart category
between 1987 and 1994 ranging from 100cc to Formula A
— scored an impressive wining record of over 95 percent in karting
competitions — two-time winner in the big ice-race Grand-Prix
Unipro du Carnaval at Quebec City in sedan racing (1993-94) —
attended Spenard David Racing School (Shannonville) in 1992 where
he placed first among 300 competing drivers in Formula 2000 — professional racing debut in 1994 at Mont-Tremblant in the F1600 Esso-
Protec series qualifying third and finishing fifth — also F2000 at
Trois-Rivières, qualified eighth and finished sixth — competed in the
1995 Esso-Protec Formula Ford, finishing fourth-place overall with
five top-five finishes including one victory

**1996 season**
finished 7th overall in the 1996 Player's/Toyota Atlantic Championship
with 3rd-place best finish at Trois-Rivières 2

**personal**
single — enjoys pool

## Bertrand Godin,
## St-Hyacinthe,
## Que., Canada   (R)
11-17-67, St-Hyacinthe, Que.

**background**
started racing go-karts in 1986 — moved to France
and competed in the French F1600 series — runner-
up in 1993 and 1994 F1600 championships — competed in
four Indy Lights races in 1995

**1996 season**
ran a four-race schedule in Indy Lights

**personal**
single

## Case Montgomery,
## Salinas, Calif.
01-04-66, Riverside, Calif.

### background
highest finishing Atlantic competitor in 1996 who is returning to the series — started racing career with a track record in Russell Racing School in 1989 — Russell Championship Race Series champion 1990 and 1991 — raced in Fastrak Competition 1991 and 1992 — competed in occasional Atlantic races 1990 to 1993 — 1994 USAC/Russell Triple Crown Series champion, with two poles and one victory — stunned veteran series observers and insiders alike with a fourth-place Atlantic Championship finish in 1995 with 114 points in only nine races — finished in the top-five in seven events with third-place outings at Montreal, Trois-Rivières (1), and Vancouver; second-place at Trois-Rivières (2); and a flag-to-flag triumph in the season finale at Laguna Seca — awarded the Michael Rosen trophy for outstanding performance

### 1996 season
finished fourth in the Player's/Toyota Atlantic Championship with 129 points — 11 top-10 finishes in 12 races including a flag-to-flag victory at Long Beach, and race runner-up showings at Milwaukee, Toronto, and Laguna Seca — also visited the podium at Mid-Ohio — scored the fastest race lap at Toronto

### personal
married (Lisa) — enjoys golf and Jessy, their two year-old yellow Labrador

## Joao Barbosa,
## Valongo,Portugal(R)
03-03-75, Rebordosa-Paredes, Portugal

### background
began competitive racing in go-karts — won his first karting event in 1987 in the Portuguese National Kart Championship Youth Category — won the 1988 Portuguese National Kart Championship Youth Category and 1988 Portugal Kart Cup Youth Category championships — two-time Portuguese National Kart Championship Junior Category (1989-90) — 1989 Portugal Kart Cup Junior champion — captured the 1990 GP Hong Kong Kart Junior title — finished fourth place in the 1990 Pre-World Kart series (Lonato Junior Category) and eighth place in the Le Mans Junior division of the European Kart championship — finished third in the 1991 World Kart Championship of Formula A in Le Mans — fourth place in 1992 World Kart Championship of Formula Super A in Ugento — began formula car racing in 1993 and finished third place in the Portuguese Formula Ford Championship — 1994 Portuguese National Formula Ford champion — 1995 Italian Formula Europa Boxer National Champion

### 1996 season
finished second-place overall in the Italian Formula 3 Championship and was named "Best Rookie of the Season" — participated in Formula One test session with Scuderia Minardi on Oct. 26, 1996

### personal
single

## Steve Knapp,
## Salem, Wis. (R)
04-04-64, Cokato, Minn.

### background
began his racing career at age 14 by becoming solely responsible for preparing his father's two-car race team — named 1978 "Land of Lakes Region" SCCA "Mechanic of the Year," the youngest recipient in SCCA history — worked as chief mechanic for the family operated multi-car Pro Super Vee team during his final years of high school — hired as a Formula Vee mechanic by Curtis Farley of C.F. Engines in Manhattan, Kan., in 1982 — built engines which won the SCCA Road Atlanta Formula Vee National Championships for 1983, 1984, and 1985 — began driving Formula Vees while working for C.F. Engines — named Kansas Region SCCA "Driver of the Year" in 1984 — moved to Antioch, Ill., in 1985 to build Super Vee and Sports 2000 engines with Bertils Race Engines — won the 1986 Sports 2000 Pro Series championship along with being the Ohio Triple Crown Winner, and the Chicago Region SCCA "Driver of the Year" — successfully defended his S2000 crown and won the 1987 S2000 Pro Series — also competed in Super Vee at the 1987 Dallas Grand Prix, where he finished seventh — ran for Adrian Reynard in 1988 and assisted in the U.S. development program for the new Reynard FF1600 and FF2000 cars — worked for Carl Haas running Mario and Michael Andretti's Indy Car Development and Test team between 1989 and 1991

### 1996 season
captured the 1996 U.S. Pro Formula Ford 2000 Championship with seven consecutive poles and four wins

### personal
father, Jerry, is former Formula Vee driver — Miller Milling Company based in Minneapolis, Minn., one of the largest U. S. millers of wheat for the pasta industry, is Knapp's primary sponsor — Knapp will continue his ongoing responsibility as Driver Development Coach and engineer for the team's U.S. FF2000 program — married to wife Bobbi, they also run Elite Engines, preparing winning power plants for many of the top FF 2000 and FF 1600 professional and amateur racers across the country — one child (Logan)

< 113 >

## Anthony Lazzaro, Acworth, Ga.
08-26-66, Charleston, S.C.

*Anthony Lazzaro* (signature)

### background
"grass roots" racing background spanning over 12 years — won five World Karting Association national championships (1987-89, 1991-92) — three-time World Karting Association world champion (1988-89, 1991) -1993 Formula Ford class champion in SCCA Valvoline National Championships — Rookie-of-the-Year in 1993 Oldsmobile Pro Series — has competed in four straight 24 Hours of Daytona (1994-97) — two-time Hooter's Formula Cup champion in 1994/1995

### 1996 season
finished an impressive sixth place in the Atlantic championship despite only competing in 10 races, and a total season budget of less than $65,000 — won in his fourth Atlantic start at Milwaukee — claimed seven top-10 finishes including fourth place at Vancouver, fifth place at Nazareth, and sixth place at Mid-Ohio — 1996 recipient of the Jovy Marcelo Sportsman Award — signed by Phillips Motorsports, of Clackamas, Ore., during the off-season to run for the Platinum Sound Racing Team, as its lead driver in the 1997 KOOL/Toyota Atlantic Championship with sponsorship from SC&T of Phoenix, Ariz.
1997 season: finished fifth in class (GTS-3) at the Rolex 24 Hours of Daytona in a Porsche 911 with Alex Job Racing — finished second place in  the "Sport class" in the IMSA Endurance Championship behind the wheel of a BMW 328si with Franz Blam Racing

### personal
10 years of extensive automotive mechanics background, primarily with BMW — married (Marcie), two children (Cory, Ansley)

## Eric Lang, New York, N.Y.
07-29-62, Minneapolis, Minn.

*Eric Lang* (signature)

### background
began racing in 1981 SCCA Formula Ford National championship finishing fifth-place overall — moved to SCCA Formula Atlantic in 1992 and finished second-place in the Northeast section — ran in British Formula 3 Championship 1983-84, finishing sixth-place overall in 1983 — moved up to British Formula 3000 Championship in 1985 — returned to North America in 1987 and ran two years in HFC Formula Atlantic series — finished fourth-place in 1987 — stepped away from racing at end of 1988 Formula Atlantic season — returned to Atlantic competition in 1995 following a six-year absence — finished 10th-place overall in Player's/Toyota Atlantic Championship with a season best fifth-place at Nazareth and five top-10 showings in 11 races

### 1996 season
contested entire 12-race Atlantic season and finished eighth-place overall with 60 points, scored six top-10 finishes including a season-best sixth place at Toronto

### personal
single — vintage motorcycle collector — enjoys deep sea fishing, skiing, and windsurfing

## Jeret Schroeder, Vineland, N.J.
11-13-69, Queens, N.Y.

*Jeret Schroeder* (signature)

### background
second-year Atlantic driver and lead driver for the P.P.I. MCI KOOL/Toyota Atlantic race team — began racing career when he attended Bob Bondurant Racing School at Sears Point International Raceway (Sonoma, Calif.) as a gift following his graduation from St. Augustine's Preparatory School in Richland, N.J., in 1988 — raced SCCA Formula Ford in 1989 — named South Jersey region's Rookie-of-the-Year in 1990 — finished fifth-place in 1992 Valvoline Run-Offs — began pro racing in 1993 with USAC Formula Ford 2000 East Championship where he won his first pole in only his second race at Indianapolis Raceway Park — forced to sit out the remainder of '93 season with leg and feet injuries following an accident at I.R.P. — competed in Formula Ford Festival at Brands Hatch, England, in 1994 — finished fourth place in USAC FF2000 National Championship, scoring seven top-10 finishes — 1995  U.S. Pro Formula Ford 2000 Champion — won four races enroute to the title (New Hampshire, Watkins Glen, Road Atlanta, and Mid-Ohio) — one of only two Americans to compete in the finals of the 1995 British Formula Ford Festival

### 1996 season
finished fifth place (77 points) in the 1996 Player's/Toyota Atlantic Championship with Lynx Racing — scored race runner-up honors at Montreal and Mid-Ohio — also visited the podium at Laguna Seca — two-time fastest race lap leader (Long Beach and Mid-Ohio)
1997 season: also competing in the Indy Racing League (IRL) with McCormack Motorsports

### personal
single — skiing, fishing, hunting, and cooking — rates Jacques Villeneuve as his favorite driver "hopes to follow in his footsteps" — personal goal is to compete in the Indianapolis 500

## David Pook,
## Long Beach, Calif.
09-04-71, Long Beach, Calif.

### background
began racing go-karts at age eight, continuing to compete in regional and national karting competitions through 1989 — participated in the Skip Barber and Jim Russell Racing Schools where he won 42% and 74% respectively, of the school races he started in 1990 — also competed in four Barber-Saab Pro Series events in 1990 — ran 11 of 12 Barber-Saab Pro Series races in 1991 finishing ninth-place overall — ran 15 out of 16 events in England's 1992 Formula Vauxhall Lotus Championship finishing 11th overall — also finished third place in the 1992 Del Mar Grand Prix season-ending Barber-Saab Pro Series race — ran a March Wildcat Indy Lights car at Laguna Seca in 1993, finishing first in class and 13th place overall — ran a six-race Indy Lights schedule in 1994 with a season best fourth place at Milwaukee — 1995 SCCA Run offs Formula Continental National Champion — finished in fifth place in the 1995 SCCA/USAC Formula 2000 Pro Championship — recipient of a 1995 Human Performance International SCCA Performance Enhancement Scholarship

### 1996 season
entered Player's/Toyota Atlantic events at Long Beach, Road America, Vancouver and Laguna Seca, scored a season best eighth place at Road America

### personal
single — enjoys go-karting, surfing and physical conditioning

## Kenny Wilden,
## Burlington,
## Ont., Canada
06-30-69, Oakville, Ont.

### background
1988 "Rookie-of-the-Year" in Honda Michelin Series — "Rookie-of-the-Year" in Player's GM Series — 1989 Grand Sports Series Champion in Firestone Firehawk Championship — won the 1992 Player's GM Series, scoring most pole positions, most lap records and most "fastest laps" — won the 24-Hour race at Mosport in 1993 in a Powell Corvette — also ran five Atlantic races in 1993, finishing second place in the final "rookie" standings behind Jacques Villeneuve — 1994 Michelin Enduro Series Champion — competed in selected Trans-Am races between 1995-96

### personal
engaged (Marie Campbell) — enjoys downhill skiing, hockey, and watersports — former Ski Patrol member

## Tony Ave,
## Indianapolis, Ind.
11-10-68, Duluth, Minn.

### background
1991 SCCA S-2000 June Sprints champion — won 1992 Oldsmobile Pro Series Championship with five victories and four poles — competed in 1992 Formula Ford Festival in Brands Hatch, England — ran two Oldsmobile Pro Series races in 1993 winning two poles and a victory — claimed two wins and five poles in '94 North America Pro Series — test and development driver for Hoosier Tire's Formula Continental and Formula Atlantic championships — ran full Trans-Am season in 1995 with Phelon Motorsports, of Aiken, S.C. — Trans-Am season best fifth-place at Phoenix — won June Sprints Formula Atlantic title

### 1996 season
finished 15th overall in Atlantic championship despite only running in four Atlantic races — claimed a season opening victory at Homestead and fifth place at Montreal — won the pole position at Long Beach in Trans-Am competition — suffered season ending injuries during June Sprints at Road America in June, 1996

### personal
single — world class Formula One snowmobile racer — finished sixth-place in 1992 Formula One World Snowmobile Championships — 1993 Pro Sprint World Snowmobile champion — finished fifth and sixth-place, respectively in 1994-95 Formula One World Snowmobile Championships — auto and snowmobile racing consultant

## Chuck West, Sonoma,
## Calif.
09-22-66, Newport Beach, Calif.

### background
sophomore season in Atlantic competition — finished third-place overall in 1990 Skip Barber Formula Ford Championship — 1991 third-place finisher in Formula Mazda Championship and Formula Continental Regional Champion (San Francisco) — won 1992 Pro Formula Mazda Championship with five wins, including 10 podium showings — Pro Formula Mazda Eastern Champion in 1994

### 1996 season
stunned Atlantic followers in his Atlantic debut with third-place at Long Beach — continued to draw raves with a second-place showing at Road America and had a sixth-place at Laguna Seca after qualifying third — factory-backed driver for Chrysler of Mexico and its Endurance Racing Team

### personal
married (Missy), one child (Dakota) — Skip Barber Racing School instructor since 1993 — test driver for tire manufacturers including Yokohama — has worked in the television and film industries as a precision and stunt driver — enjoys water skiing and tennis — accomplished 14-year veteran in Chinese martial arts studies — holds black belt in Kung Fu — owns and manages a 12-car Formula Mazda racing program which has earned five professional and/or regional titles in the last five years.

< 115 >

**Bill Auberlen,
Redondo Beach,
Calif. (R)**

10-12-68, Redondo Beach,
Calif.

### background

13-year motocross veteran starting at age four — moved from two-wheel competition to four wheels at age 18 (1987) and became a top IMSA GTU competitor — led 24 Hrs. of Daytona in first profession-al start (1988) and finished second in GTU — scored six IMSA class victories, including the Fuji and Autopolis Japan invitational events between 1993-94 — 1994 posted three wins/ four pole positions in nine IMSA GTU races — 1995 finished second in IMSA GTS-2 championship, claiming seven poles and five victories (Sebring, Lime Rock, Texas World Speedway, Phoenix, New Orleans) — raced two Atlantic events finishing second along with having the fastest race lap at the season opener at Miami, his first ever Atlantic race

### 1996 season

ran Atlantic season opener at Homestead where he qualified second and finished fifth — competed in IMSA's GTS-2 class with the BMW factory team that won the Constructor's Championship — won the pole position at Watkins Glen
1997 season: IMSA GTS-3 winner (9th overall) in factory BMW M3 at Rolex 24 Hrs. of Daytona

### personal

single — owns/operates Auberlen Racing Concepts, tuning shop for imported and classic autos — 2nd generation IMSA driver; father, Gary, was IMSA driver and 1985 Sebring winner — designs/builds

**Cameron Binder,
Calgary,
Alta., Canada**

09-17-71, Calgary, Alta.,
Canada

### background

1992 graduate of Jim Russell Racing School (Laguna Seca) - two-year veteran of Canada's Hankook Formula 1600 championship (1993-94) - 1994 Hankook Formula 1600 titlist behind five victories and two runner-up finishes - competed in two Atlantic races in 1994, finishing 10th at Vancouver and 12th at Laguna Seca - raced in both 1995 Indy Lights and the Player's/Toyota Atlantic Championship - ran four Atlantic races with a season best 10th-place at Trois-Rivières (2) and finished seventh in final C2 standings

### 1996 season

ran first full Atlantic schedule with newly formed Binder Motorsports - finished 13th overall with three top-10 finishes with season-best sixth place at Vancouver

### personal

single - enjoys water skiing, snowboarding, golf, and hockey

**Michael David,
Corona, Calif.**

10-10-72, Orange, Calif.

### background

began competitive racing at age 9 on BMX bicycles — accomplished go-kart racer in 100cc and 125cc Shifter Kart classes in International Karting Federation (1986-92) — raced three years (1992-94) in Skip Barber Ford series — finished 10th in first career Atlantic race at Laguna Seca Raceway in 1994 — 1995 C2 runner-up with 141 points and tied for 16th place (22 points) in overall Atlantic championship despite a limit-ed schedule, winning four of the final five C2 races

### 1996 season

competed in a new PDR Enterprises-prepared Ralt RT-41 where he scored consistent top-10 finishes including fifth place at Long Beach and fourth-place qualifying at Road America — completed a two-day course at Florida's Human Performance International in Oct. 1996

### personal

married (Rochelle)

**Ted Sahley,
Cleveland, Ohio**

12-27-72, Cleveland, Ohio

### background

entering his second season of Atlantic competition and has been named lead driver in 1997 for Mike Shank Racing Services — has competed in 20 career Skip Barber Formula Ford races — ran five races in 1995 U.S. Formula Ford 2000 National Championship — finished fifth place in the 1995 SCCA Run-offs in Formula Ford 2000

### 1996 season

raced in six Atlantic events in the C2 division races — scored C2 vic-tories at Homestead, Milwaukee, and Mid-Ohio — finished second and third place, respectively at Trios-Rivières 1 & 2 — fourth place in C2 season standings with 106 points.

### personal

single — graduated from the University of Florida in 1996 with a BA in advertising & marketing — interested in business ventures in the hotel business industry — bilingual in Spanish and English — mother from Lima, Peru

### Robert Sollenskog, Antioch, Ill.
09-22-70, Vasteros, Sweden

*Robert Sollenskog*

**background**
first racing experiences were in 100cc go-karts at age 16 where he scored podium finishes in 16 of 20 race starts — personally invited by Bertil Roos, a long time family friend, to attend the Bertil Roos Grand Prix Racing School in 1990 — raced a Citation in Formula Continental 2000 Class in the Central Division of the SCCA in 1991 — claimed nine podium finishes and four wins in 13 outings and named "Rookie-of-the-Year" — ran limited Formula Atlantic events in 1992 — changed roles in 1993 and worked as chief mechanic for Anthony Lazzaro in Oldsmobile Pro Series, guiding Lazzaro to three victories — also competed in selected S2000 races in '93 where he finished third-place in the Valvoline Run-Offs — first pro series was the North American Pro Series in 1994 and scored three podium finishes with one victory, and named NAPS "Rookie-of-the-Year" — competed at Montreal and Mid-Ohio in 1995 Player's/Toyota Atlantic Championship

**1996 season**
11th place in 1996 Player's/Toyota Atlantic Championship with 51 points behind six top-10 finishes in 11 races — best finishes were sixth place at Toronto and Trois-Rivières

**personal**
former world ranked junior snow ski racer — enjoys water and snow skiing, and biking — married (Jacqueline), one child (Robert Julian)

### David Cutler, Medina, Wash.
03-03-42, Lansing, Mich.

*Dave Cutler*

**background**
relative newcomer to racing with two years of experience in the Russell Championship Series and USAC Russell Triple Crown Series in 1994 and 1995 — also ran '95 Star Mazda Series

**1996 season**
raced in 10 Atlantic events with Sandy Dells Racing teammate and Atlantic standout Case Montgomery — scored season-best 12th place showings at Homestead and Milwaukee

**personal**
software engineer and executive with Microsoft — avid skier and squash player — member of National Academy of Engineering — single, three children (Lisa, Tim, Keith)

### Mark Tague, Laguna Hills, Calif. (R)
08-09-54, Inglewood, Calif.

**background**
first year Atlantic driver running with Chuck West's World Speed Motorsports team — started competitive racing in go-karts, and ran regional karting events 1994-96 — attended Jim Russell Racing School at Laguna Seca in 1994 and finished eighth place in the Russell School Championship — finished third place in the 1995 Russell School Championship

**1996 season**
ran in Star Series Formula Mazda Championship, finishing third place overall

**personal**
married (Laurie) — Certified Public Accountant (CPA) — CEO of Altec — co-founder of "Platinum Software," a software company which he took public in 1992

< 117 >

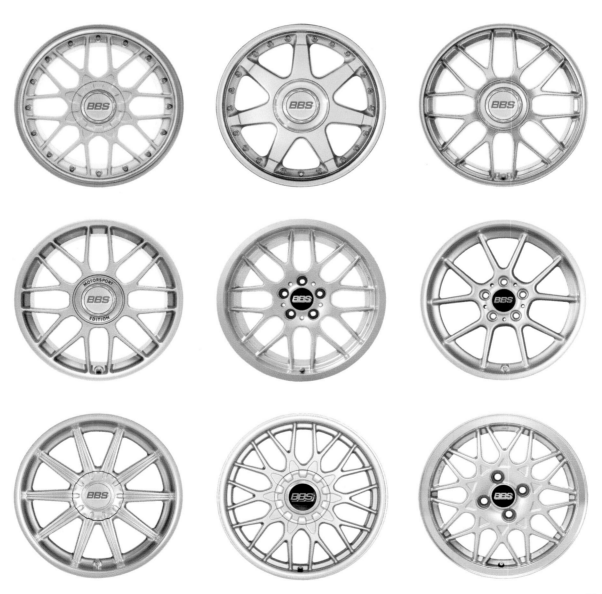

Doug Shierson

## NOWHERE WITHOUT THE TEAMS

Although Atlantic has always rightly focused its attentions upon its drivers, those drivers would never have gone anywhere without the entrants and teams behind them. Because Atlantic's very nature as a training category means it is a transient arena through which drivers constantly pass on their way to somewhere else, it is these teams that provide the formula with its grounding stability.

This remains as true today as anytime in the past, and the honor roll of supporters with more than just passing interest in the series includes names like Bill Brack, Chris Harrison, Carl Haas, Doug Shierson, Fred Opert, Pierre Phillips, Jon Norman, Allan McCall, Rick Shea, Tom Gloy, Jim and Barbara Trueman, Brian Robertson, Dennis Eade, Stuart Moore, Alister McNeill, Bill Fickling, Dwayne Anderson, Angelo Ferro, John Della Penna, Joe Sposato (who started his record 100th Atlantic race as a driver in 1997), Peter Greenfield, Sandy Dells and, most recently, the Lynx Racing duo of Peggy Haas and Jackie Doty. Without them, none of this would ever have happened.

Pierre Phillips (center)
with drivers Tony Rouff and Geoff Brabham

Alan McCall and Tom Gloy

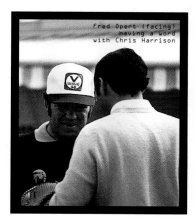

Fred Opert (facing) having a word with Chris Harrison

Chris Harrison

Peggy Haas

< 119 >

## Lazzaro Takes Season Opener

With the addition of new co-title sponsor, KOOL, a bold new logo, and the excitement of the impending season, the KOOL/Toyota Atlantic Championship series kicked off its 1997 schedule at the Metro-Dade Motorsports Complex, in Homestead, Fla. Defending Champion Patrick Carpentier was there in full-force - but for the first time in seven races, he would not be the man everyone feared, having graduated as the new driver for Team Alumax / Bettenhausen Motorsports' Championship Auto Racing Teams (CART) effort.

For the drivers and fans of the 1997 KOOL/Toyota Atlantic Championship there would be no clear cut favorite for the title.

It certainly started out that way as Chuck West, perhaps not blessed with the biggest of racing budgets, but with no shortage of talent, took the pole in his Ralt RT-41. His qualifying lap around the six-turn 1.4-mile course (CART and Indy Lights drove on the four turn 1.51-mile oval that weekend) set a new track record for Atlantic series cars, at 41.564 seconds (121.25 miles per hour).

The Skip Barber Racing School instructor was hoping to have his way in the race, however it was not to be for West, who led from the pole but touched wheels with Lynx Racing rookie Memo Gidley and crashed out of contention on the ninth lap. He was not injured.

Gidley then assumed the lead for six laps before running off course. Case Montgomery passed him and appeared headed for his third career Atlantic victory in as many seasons. Montgomery was cruising comfortably, leading 32 laps, until he heard some disturbing noises popping out of his engine, especially on the restart after a yellow caution flag was dropped for Leo Parente's disabled vehicle.

"I thought I had this thing covered until I heard a couple of pops," said Montgomery. "I hoped it wasn't what I thought. It was the engine and it just got worse. I tried to be smooth and I thought there was a hope to keep Memo behind me. Well, he got a great run through the third turn, and though I thought about forcing him to the far outside, I knew it probably wouldn't work. I tried to get into his slipscreen and I almost had him beat in Turn Five. It took all I had to save the car."

< 121 >

While Montgomery saved his misfiring car, and Gidley got past, another driver proved that patience is a virtue and made his move as well. Anthony Lazzaro, of Acworth, Ga., had kept pace with Montgomery and Gidley all day. He decided to make his move on Lap 48, just two laps from the finish.

The result was Lazzaro's second career Atlantic win, and a $22,000 pay day – $20,000 for first and $1,000 each for his "KOOL Move of the Race" and "Yokohama Now You've Got Control" awards.

"The pass for the lead was uneventful because he (Montgomery) was a sitting duck," admitted Lazzaro. "His engine sounded like a popcorn popper."

Lazzaro was not without his own aggravations during the race. "The car popped out of fifth gear because my arm was rubbing so hard against the lever when I was holding the steering wheel. That cost me time on two occasions."

But it didn't cost him at the most important time. "Winning the first race of the year gives the entire Platinum Sound / BG Products team momentum," added Lazzaro. "Phillips Motorsports did an outstanding job, and our winter testing seems to have been so worthwhile now."

Gidley finished second and picked up the $1,000 KOOL Rookie Challenge prize. In addition, he was credited with the fastest race lap, at 41.694 seconds (120.88 mph). Third went to the struggling Montgomery. The C2 winner (a competitive class for older Atlantic cars – Swift-DB4 and Reynard 89H to 93H) was hometown driver Joaquin DeSoto.

< 123 >

POLE POSITION
Chuck West

RESULTS
Anthony Lazzaro
Memo Gidley
Case Montgomery
Joao Barbosa
Bertrand Godin
Steve Knapp
Bill Auberlen
Alexandre Tagliani
Eric Lang
Cam Binder

| STANDINGS | POINTS |
|---|---|
| Anthony Lazzaro | 20 |
| Memo Gidley | 16 |
| Case Montgomery | 15 |
| Joao Barbosa | 12 |
| Bertrand Godin | 11 |
| Steve Knapp | 10 |
| Bill Auberlen | 9 |
| Alexandre Tagliani | 8 |
| Eric Lang | 7 |
| Cam Binder | 6 |

| C2 | POINTS |
|---|---|
| Joaquin DeSoto | 21 |
| Mike Sauce | 16 |
| Dan Vosloo | 14 |
| Greg Harrington | 12 |

| | |
|---|---|
| KOOL Move of the Race | Anthony Lazzaro |
| KOOL Rookie Challenge | Memo Gidley |
| Yokohama "Now You've Got Control" | Anthony Lazzaro |

< 125 >

## Tagliani collects first win

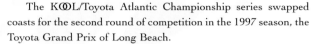

The K(OO)L/Toyota Atlantic Championship series swapped coasts for the second round of competition in the 1997 season, the Toyota Grand Prix of Long Beach.

Canadian Alexandre Tagliani held off a late race challenge from Anthony Lazzaro to post his first Atlantic win after a late caution set up a two-lap showdown. Lazzaro was able to hang on to second from a hard-charging Bill Auberlen. Joao Barbosa was also in the hunt, on Auberlen's tail for a solid fourth.

California native Case Montgomery held the pole position and led the 36-car field cleanly through Turn One after the signature Atlantic series beginning – the standing start. Race pace was short lived however, when the yellow flag immediately came out for Michael David who stalled on course and was forced to retire from the race with a broken axle.

Montgomery was quickly challenged on the lap five restart by Anthony Lazzaro. Lazzaro won the battle and passed him through Turn One. Player's Alexandre Tagliani followed Lazzaro's lead and moved Montgomery to third. For Montgomery, things only got worse from there, as he banged wheels with fourth place Alex Barron and spun on the same lap.

"Anthony got a really good jump on the restart," said Montgomery. "He got on the power and got a wheel on me and I thought 'Well, he got a great jump, I'll just stay right here.' Then going into Turn One, two cars got by me and as I turned in, I got hit by Barron. From that point on, the car was terrible under braking."

The battle for control of the race then pitted Lazzaro against Tagliani. Tagliani took the lead on lap seven, before the race was red-flagged for a track-blocking incident involving Tagliani's teammate, Bertrand Godin.

Godin made contact with the Turn Eight apex exiting the hairpin on lap 11 and came to a stop facing the flow of traffic. In an attempt to continue, he drove in a counter-track direction and Cam Binder unavoidably hit the Player's car while exiting Turn Eight. Jeret Schroeder compounded the problem as he made nose-to-tail contact with Binder and Turn Eight became impassable, bringing out the red flag to clear the track.

< 127 >

Tagliani was able to maintain his lead on the lap 12 restart while Ave and Auberlen made moves to pick up a respective third and fifth a little farther back. Ave's progress was short-lived when he was forced to retire with over-heating problems and the action was again cut short as quickly as it had begun as the caution was brought out for 20th-place Bob Siska when he spun and was collected by Marcelo Gaffoglio. One additional yellow flag period kept Tagliani's challengers (Lazzaro, Bill Auberlen and Joao Barbosa) close and set up the final dash to the checkered flag.

They went four wide into Turn One when the green flag flew on lap 28, yet Tagliani held on to the lead, as Memo Gidley and Montgomery battled for fifth. Montgomery, who had valiantly battled his way back to fifth after his first-lap spin, spun again in Turn Six, and Gidley, struggling with gearbox gremlins all day, slowed as more internals let go. This moved Steve Knapp to fifth and Chuck West into sixth at the checkered flag.

Tagliani finished 1.4529 seconds ahead of his closest challenger and collected $20,000 in his first career Atlantic series victory. Lazzaro accepted the second place trophy and maintained his first place points position. Third place Auberlen took the remaining honors, adding $2,000 to his winnings with the "KOOL Move of the Race" and the "Yokohama Now You've Got Control" awards, as well as the $1,000 KOOL Rookie Challenge award.

### POLE POSITION
Case Montgomery

### RESULTS
Alexandre Tagliani
Anthony Lazzaro
Bill Auberlen
Joao Barbosa
Steve Knapp
Chuck West
Memo Gidley
Charles Nearburg
Eric Lang
Case Montgomery

### STANDINGS POINTS
| | |
|---|---|
| Anthony Lazzaro | 36 |
| Alexandre Tagliani | 29 |
| Memo Gidley | 25 |
| Joao Barbosa | 24 |
| Bill Auberlen | 23 |
| Case Montgomery | 22 |
| Steve Knapp | 21 |
| Eric Lang | 14 |
| Bertrand Godin | 11 |
| Chuck West | 11 |

### C2 POINTS
| | |
|---|---|
| Dan Vosloo | 28 |
| Joaquin DeSoto | 21 |
| Frank Allers | 21 |
| Buddy Brundo | 16 |
| Mike Sauce | 16 |

| | |
|---|---|
| KOOL Move of the Race | Bill Auberlen |
| KOOL Rookie Challenge | Bill Auberlen |
| Yokohama "Now You've Got Control" | Bill Auberlen |

< 131 >

## Barron breaks through

Rookie Alex Barron, of Vista, Calif., sprinted wire-to-wire from the pole in his Lynx Racing / Victory Circle Racing Ralt RT-41 to capture his first career KOOL/Toyota Atlantic Championship race at the Bosch Spark Plug Grand Prix presented by Toyota. While Barron led comfortably in only his third career Atlantic start, the victory was a familiar one for the Lynx team who posted their third straight victory at Nazareth. Case Montgomery, Alexandre Tagliani and Steve Knapp battled for the runner-up spot in the closing laps at the Nazareth Speedway, and finished in that order.

Barron, running strong all weekend, got the jump at the drop of the green flag and never looked back, despite five caution period restarts.

"The restarts were challenging," said Barron, about the one-mile track that goes uphill as cars approach the start-finish line. "I'm a little inexperienced on restarts. We had to keep the momentum going."

The first caution of the race flew on lap seven when Stuart Crow made hard contact with the wall entering Turn Four. On the lap 15 restart, Barron was followed closely by teammate and fellow rookie, Memo Gidley, who had made it an all-Lynx Racing front row in qualifying. Tagliani, Knapp and Anthony Lazzaro followed the lead duo in a steady battle that soon took the lead pack into lapped traffic.

On lap 23, Mark Tague dropped down the track in Turn One as ninth-placed Robert Sollenskog came up to lap him. Sollenskog tried to avoid a collision, but the pair touched and Tague lost control, spinning backwards into the wall and bringing out the next caution. Sollenskog was fortunate to continue without losing position, suffering only a bent front wing.

< 133 >

On the ensuing lap 33 restart, Lazzaro moved outside to pass Gidley, who had just moved outside of Tagliani and a lapped car. Four-wide into turn one, Lazzaro had nearly made it by, but made contact with the right front wheel of Gidley's car. Lazzaro spun into the Turn One infield and Gidley stopped with a damaged suspension after making light contact with the outside wall.

"It was just a racing incident," said Lazzaro. "I just ran out of room. It's unfortunate because it hurts us in the championship."

The late race shootout was set up when C2 leader Joaquin DeSoto lost control in Turn Four of the one-mile oval and collected the second-place C2 car of Greg Harrington before hitting the wall. Harrington was able to make repairs during the lap 45 caution and went on to win the C2 class.

When the green flag fell on lap 52 of the 60-lap event, Barron pulled away while the real battle ensued for second, with Montgomery challenging Tagliani and a hard-charging Knapp soon to join the fray.

Knapp drove in hard to pass Montgomery and Tagliani in Turn Two on lap 58, but, Knapp got loose in Turn Three and Montgomery swept past both drivers to claim second place.

"Steve got super loose, almost sideways, but he saved it," said Montgomery. "Tagliani had to check up for him and I just kept my foot in it and got around. It was great."

In the end, Barron took home $20,000 for his first Atlantic series victory. He also claimed the $1,000 KOOL Rookie Challenge award. Montgomery collected second place, along with a $1,000 bonus for winning the "KOOL Move of the Race" and $1,000 for winning the "Yokohama Now You've Got Control" award.

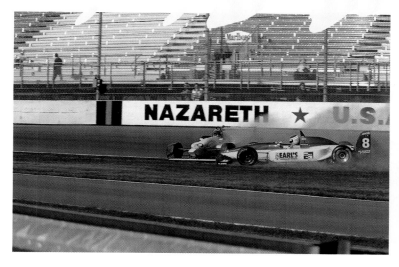

< 135 >

### POLE POSITION
Alex Barron

### RESULTS
Alex Barron
Case Montgomery
Alexandre Tagliani
Steve Knapp
Tony Ave
David Pook
Michael David
Jeret Schroeder
Robert Sollenskog
Bertrand Godin

| STANDINGS | POINTS |
|---|---|
| Alexandre Tagliani | 43 |
| Case Montgomery | 38 |
| Anthony Lazzaro | 36 |
| Steve Knapp | 33 |
| Joao Barbosa | 28 |
| Memo Gidley | 25 |
| Bill Auberlen | 23 |
| Alex Barron | 22 |
| Eric Lang | 19 |
| Bertrand Godin | 17 |

| C2 | POINTS |
|---|---|
| Joaquin DeSoto | 36 |
| Greg Harrington | 32 |
| Dan Vosloo | 28 |
| Frank Allers | 21 |
| Buddy Brundo | 16 |

KOOL Move of the Race — Case Montgomery

KOOL Rookie Challenge — Alex Barron

Yokohama "Now You've Got Control" — Case Montgomery

< 137 >

# Barron goes two-for-two

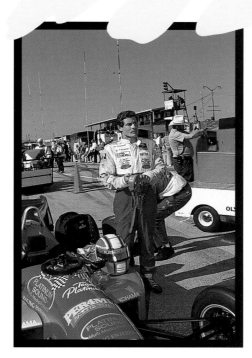

Rookie Alex Barron captured his second consecutive and second career KOOL /Toyota Atlantic Championship race from the pole at the Milwaukee Mile. In just his fourth career Atlantic start, Barron held the lead for most of the 60-lap event, but the remainder of the top ten was not decided until the checkered flag fell.

"The car had a bad push at first, but then the tires came in, and I was able to balance it with the bars so the car was really good in the race," said Barron. "The first green was so long that I was a little happy to have a few yellows so that I could rest. I'm surprised and happy to have won two races in a row from the pole, but there are still a lot of races to go, and our philosophy is to take them one at a time."

Barron took the lead at the drop of the green flag and was challenged early by outside pole sitter Tony Ave. Ave, however, soon had to fend off David Pook, who sneaked from his fourth place starting spot into contention. Pook took over second place on lap 20 following an exciting multi-lap dual with Ave.

Posturing among the 29-car field was the mode of the day. Jeret Schroeder battled Anthony Lazzaro for fifth place throughout much of the early going. The pair, led by Lazzaro, moved past Bertrand Godin on lap 12. Memo Gidley, charging hard since lap one, also squeezed past Godin and joined the battle for fourth after starting 11th.

< 139 >

The race was slowed on lap 34 after Sergei Szortyka made nose-to-tail contact with Howie Liebengood. Szortyka spun and continued. Liebengood drove to the pits but he was done for the day.

Racing resumed on lap 41, and despite the battles for fifth place among Lazzaro, Schroeder and Godin, the winner of the spot turned out to be Chuck West, who had stormed toward the front from his 18th starting position. West's run on the field was halted on lap 54 when Michael David spun between Turns Three and Four, resulting in hard contact with the wall. David was uninjured, but West's hopes of catching Ave and earning fourth place were dashed as this yellow ended the day's green flag racing action.

"Tony had just slipped coming off Four and I had him, but the yellow flew," said West. "It was a great race for my second oval. I passed cars high and low in the same lap."

As the race finished under caution, Barron crossed the finish line ahead of Pook. Barron's results brought him the $20,000 first place prize, as well as the $1,000 KOOL Rookie Challenge award, for the second week in a row. Gidley was awarded third place, the $1,000 bonus for the "KOOL Move of the Race" award, and another $1,000 for winning the "Yokohama Now You've Got Control" award.

< 141 >

*round* 4

POLE POSITION
Alex Barron

RESULTS
Alex Barron
David Pook
Memo Gidley
Tony Ave
Chuck West
Anthony Lazzaro
Bertrand Godin
Jeret Schroeder
Stuart Crow
Alexandre Tagliani

| STANDINGS | POINTS |
|---|---|
| Alexandre Tagliani | 49 |
| Anthony Lazzaro | 46 |
| Alex Barron | 44 |
| Memo Gidley | 39 |
| Case Montgomery | 38 |
| Steve Knapp | 37 |
| Joao Barbosa | 31 |
| Tony Ave | 28 |
| Bertrand Godin | 26 |
| David Pook | 26 |

| C2 | POINTS |
|---|---|
| Joaquin DeSoto | 57 |
| Greg Harrington | 32 |
| Howie Liebengood | 30 |
| Dan Vosloo | 28 |
| Frank Allers | 21 |

KOOL Move of the Race   Memo Gidley

KOOL Rookie Challenge   Alex Barron

Yokohama "Now You've Got Control"   Memo Gidley

< 143 >

# Hometown hero godin gets the gold

Rookie Bertrand Godin, of nearby St. Hyacinthe, Que., won his first career KOOL/Toyota Atlantic Championship race at Montreal's 2.747-mile Gilles-Villeneuve Circuit in his Player's Forsythe Racing Ralt RT-40. Godin led 26 of the 27 laps, sprinting to finish 4.164 seconds ahead of fellow rookie Alex Barron.

"This is a dream come true," said an ecstatic Godin. "It's wonderful to win in front of our home crowd, in front of the Player's people."

The victory capped a weekend that saw Godin shatter the existing track qualifying record, held previously by fellow Canadian, CART FedEx Championship driver Patrick Carpentier. Godin's time of 1:38.687 easily eclipsed Carpentier's 1:40.373 set last June.

At the standing start, Case Montgomery and Tony Ave were quickest off the line, slipping past a wheel-spinning Godin going into Turn One. Godin got back by Ave and kept heavy pressure on Montgomery throughout the opening lap, and regained the lead on the next circuit when the two drivers banged wheels on the front straightaway.

Meanwhile, Barron watched and waited for any opening that might occur. His patience was rewarded and Barron passed Montgomery on lap 10. However, Montgomery did not go away and continually pressured Barron. Jeret Schroeder soon made it a three-way battle after sneaking up from seventh on the starting grid.

Schroeder, whose brakes were fading, made nose-to-tail contact with Montgomery on lap 11, and went spinning into the Turn 15 gravel pit. Montgomery was able to recover after getting sideways and maintained his third position. Unfortunately his gearbox had taken a direct hit in the incident and he was forced to retire on lap 15 with gear-linkage problems.

"Alex Barron, Case Montgomery and I were battling for second place as we went into the last chicane," said Schroeder. "Unfortunately, three laps into the race, my brakes started fading and by then they were completely gone. There was nowhere to go and I hit Case."

Godin had stretched his lead over Barron to more than seven seconds in the early laps, but it had been cut to less than four seconds by lap 21. Barron was unchallenged for second place, with his next closest competitor, outside polesitter Kenny Wilden, almost 23 seconds behind, followed by Lang, Gidley, Sollenskog and Lazzaro.

< 145 >

Chuck West, who set the fastest race lap at 1:38.864 and had been charging through the field with Joao Barbosa, experienced brake failure going into Turn 10 and plowed into the back of Barbosa. West was done for the day, but a trip to the pits returned Barbosa and he managed to finish in 19th - disappointing, but still not bad considering his last-place start from the pits.

Barron closed the gap on Godin to within two seconds on lap 24, and was within 1.13 seconds when the white flag flew. Yet, the winner's purse went to Godin, who held his lead to prevail over Barron. Memo Gidley finished third to complete the season's first all-rookie podium.

"This was the best race I've ever had," said Barron, who took the Atlantic points lead. "It was very physical, with lots of bumping and jostling going on, and of course it was very long, so you really had to maintain your concentration. This is a very technical track, and there are a lot of tricks and things to learn so you can go fast... I'm very happy with our results, and happy to be leading the championship. I think we're in the hunt now, and instead of focusing on learning, we'll be focusing on winning races."

Godin took home $20,000 for his victory and an additional $1,000 for the KⓄOL Rookie Challenge award. Godin also took the early lead in the Player's Challenge, which recognized the efforts of the 15 highest-placing drivers who earned the most points in the series' Canadian Atlantic events. Joao Barbosa was awarded $1,000 for the "KⓄOL Move of the Race" and $1,000 for the "Yokohama Now You've Got Control" bonus for his spirited run through the field and 19th place finish.

< 147 >

## POLE POSITION
Bertrand Godin

## RESULTS
Bertrand Godin
Alex Barron
Memo Gidley
Eric Lang
Anthony Lazzaro
David Pook
Robert Sollenskog
Ted Sahley
Leo Parente
Cam Binder

| STANDINGS | POINTS |
|---|---|
| Alex Barron | 60 |
| Anthony Lazzaro | 57 |
| Memo Gidley | 53 |
| Alexandre Tagliani | 49 |
| Bertrand Godin | 48 |
| Case Montgomery | 38 |
| Steve Knapp | 37 |
| David Pook | 36 |
| Eric Lang | 36 |
| Tony Ave | 33 |

| C2 | POINTS |
|---|---|
| Joaquin DeSoto | 67 |
| James Irvin | 36 |
| Greg Harrington | 32 |
| Frank Allers | 33 |
| Howie Liebengood | 30 |

| KOOL Move of the Race | Joao Barbosa |
|---|---|
| KOOL Rookie Challenge | Bertrand Godin |
| Yokohama "Now You've Got Control" | Joao Barbosa |

| PLAYER'S CHALLENGE STANDINGS | ROUND ONE |
|---|---|
| Bertrand Godin | 22 |
| Alex Barron | 16 |
| Memo Gidley | 14 |
| Eric Lang | 12 |
| Anthony Lazzaro | 11 |

< 149 >

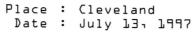

# Godin goes two in a row

After a lightning fast qualifying session afforded the Player's Forsythe Racing driver his first career Atlantic pole position, Alexandre Tagliani's luck seemed to run out. On the first of two scheduled "reconnaissance" laps before the start of the race at Cleveland's temporary circuit on Burke Lakefront Airport's runways, Tagliani's engine cover flew off and then his gearbox seized, and his day ended before it had begun.

Further drama in the pre-race procession ensued when Michael David's car burst into flames as a result of a fuel leak, and he headed for the nearest fire fighters.

The race went on without David and Tagliani, and Tagliani's Player's teammate, Bertrand Godin, took advantage of the vacant space ahead of him. Godin took the lead from Memo Gidley at Turn One, as all 28 cars made it cleanly through the first turn following the "standing start".

Several competitors found themselves spinning across the tarmac in the early going, including Barron, who spun and continued, and Pook, who spun and was finished for the day. These minor incidents paled in contrast to Robert Sollenskog's frightening impact with the Turn 8 wall. Fortunately, the nearly head-on hit was not quite as bad as it seemed – unfortunately, the promising young driver Sollenskog did sustain a season-ending left foot injury.

< 151 >

When the field resumed green flag racing on Lap 11, Godin "backed-off" the field approaching the line, causing Memo Gidley to nearly brake to a halt to avoid rear-ending him. Case Montgomery, Joao Barbosa, and Anthony Lazzaro, tried to read the move through Turn 1, but only Montgomery gained a position, which Gidley re-took on the next lap. Furious dicing behind the leader brought Alex Barron and Tony Ave into the mix by lap 15.

A lap 20 dash through Turn One saw Lynx Racing teammates Memo Gidley and Alex Barron make contact while disputing second place with Montgomery. Both Lynx cars continued, but Montgomery took advantage of the altercation and moved into second position, as Gidley fell to eleventh.

"That was perfect," said Montgomery. "I could see what was going to happen. It was as if I was not even there and was watching from overhead."

An apologetic Barron said, "I'm sorry about what happened with Memo. It's unfortunate we hit. I don't wish that on anyone, especially my teammate."

Due to time limitations imposed by the impending CART television schedule, the race ended on lap 22, affording Godin his second straight Atlantic victory and another $20,000 victory check, along with the $1,000 KOOL Rookie Challenge bonus. Montgomery held on to second position and collected the $1,000 "KOOL Move of the Race" and $1,000 "Yokohama Now You've Got Control" awards. Alex Barron captured the final podium position with his third place effort.

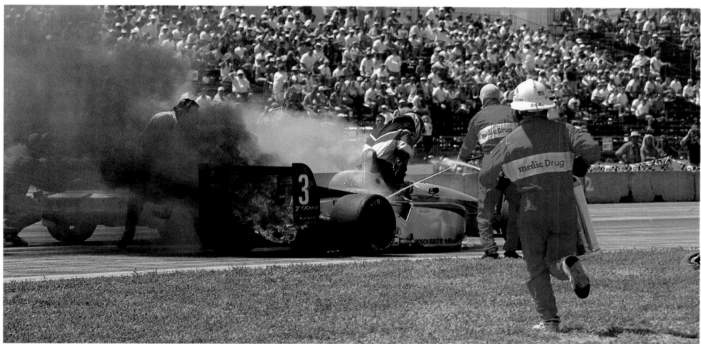

< 153 >

## POLE POSITION
Alexandre Tagliani

## RESULTS
Bertrand Godin
Case Montgomery
Alex Barron
Jeret Schroeder
Tony Ave
Chuck West
Joao Barbosa
Steve Knapp
Memo Gidley
Cam Binder

| STANDINGS | POINTS |
|---|---|
| Alex Barron | 74 |
| Bertrand Godin | 69 |
| Anthony Lazzaro | 62 |
| Memo Gidley | 60 |
| Case Montgomery | 54 |
| Alexandre Tagliani | 50 |
| Steve Knapp | 45 |
| Tony Ave | 44 |
| Joao Barbosa | 40 |
| Eric Lang | 39 |

| C2 | POINTS |
|---|---|
| Joaquin DeSoto | 88 |
| James Irvin | 52 |
| Greg Harrington | 44 |
| Howie Liebengood | 41 |
| Frank Allers | 33 |

KOOL Move of the Race — Case Montgomery

KOOL Rookie Challenge — Bertrand Godin

Yokohama "Now You've Got Control" — Case Montgomery

< 155 >

# Gidley gets his first

Rookie Memo Gidley claimed his first career KOOL /Toyota Atlantic series victory on the 1.721-mile temporary street circuit around Toronto's Exhibition Place. Gidley led the final 10 laps of the contest that ended under yellow after Greg Harrington made contact with the back-straight wall, bringing out the sixth caution of the day. Alexandre Tagliani followed in second and Case Montgomery completed the podium picture by taking third.

"I can't tell you how much I wanted this and how relaxed I am," said Gidley. The season started off well, but we've had some problems where I had to come up through the field, and that seems to have been good practice. Considering where I started, this is just fantastic. I just drove my heart out and everything clicked. Lynx Racing gave me a great opportunity. I may not have had the fastest car today, but I made some good moves and got a few lucky breaks, and here we are. I could have lucked into a win earlier in the season, but I feel like I earned this one."

Polesitter Alex Barron had led the field into Turn One following the traditional Atlantic standing start. Alexandre Tagliani began a fierce battle with Barron on lap two, but Tagliani soon had to hold off the challenges of Montgomery, who had quickly found his way to third from his eighth starting position. Yet Tagliani's persistence paid off and he passed Barron on lap 14 following a restart.

A lap 21 restart cost Barron another position as his teammate Gidley charged past him for second. Montgomery and Bill Auberlen also passed Barron later in the lap.

< 157 >

Tagliani and Gidley engaged in a wheel-to-wheel duel on the lap 25 restart, until Gidley secured the lead between Turns Seven and Eight. Again the field was slowed by a caution, but Gidley maintained his lead under Tagliani's heavy pressure when racing resumed.

Gidley led Tagliani and Montgomery to the checkered flag under caution. Joao Barbosa and Auberlen followed in fourth and fifth.

"I'm a little disappointed with third position, but it's a lot better than fourth," said Montgomery. "Since we had bad weekends at Long Beach, Milwaukee and Montreal, I really need to win to get back up in the points system, but the race ended under yellow before I could see if I could get past Alex and Memo. My hat's off to them... they were having a great show. I was hoping they might get together, or go outside, because I was just sitting in the catbird's seat, waiting for my chance."

Gidley took home $20,000 for his win and $1,000 for the "Yokohama Now You've Got Control" award. Gidley swept the KOOL award jackpot by collecting both $1,000 prizes, the KOOL Rookie Challenge and "KOOL Move of the Race."

< 159 >

POLE POSITION
Alex Barron

RESULTS
Memo Gidley
Alexandre Tagliani
Case Montgomery
Joao Barbosa
Bill Auberlen
Alex Barron
Bertrand Godin
Jeret Schroeder
Kenny Wilden
David Pook

| STANDINGS | POINTS |
|---|---|
| Alex Barron | 86 |
| Memo Gidley | 80 |
| Bertrand Godin | 78 |
| Case Montgomery | 68 |
| Alexandre Tagliani | 66 |
| Anthony Lazzaro | 62 |
| Joao Barbosa | 52 |
| Steve Knapp | 50 |
| Tony Ave | 44 |
| David Pook | 42 |

| C2 | POINTS |
|---|---|
| Joaquin DeSoto | 104 |
| James Irvin | 72 |
| Greg Harrington | 56 |
| Frank Allers | 45 |
| Howie Liebengood | 41 |

| | |
|---|---|
| K◎OL Move of the Race | Memo Gidley |
| K◎OL Rookie Challenge | Memo Gidley |
| Yokohama "Now You've Got Control" | Memo Gidley |
| MCI Fast Pace Award | Alexandre Tagliani |

PLAYER'S CHALLENGE

| STANDINGS | ROUND TWO |
|---|---|
| Memo Gidley | 34 |
| Bertrand Godin | 31 |
| Alex Barron | 28 |
| David Pook / Alexandre Tagliani | 16 |

< 161 >

## Alexandre the great

Canadian local hero and polesitter Alexandre Tagliani won the second KOOL/Toyota Atlantic Championship race of his career with a wire-to-wire victory on the 1.51-mile Trois-Rivières street circuit. Joao Barbosa finished second, followed by a feisty Alex Barron who had been giving Tagliani a mirror full throughout most of the contest.

Tagliani led the entire race that ended under yellow after Bob Thomas experienced mechanical problems and dropped oil on the track, bringing out the third caution of the day, and causing Barron to slip from second to third.

"This was a team result," said Tagliani. "The crew worked so hard and we had so many small mechanical problems. They worked all night and all weekend to resolve the problems. We started the race with another battery to make sure we would be able to finish the 50 laps. The brake problems I had during the race were helped by the caution periods. With all the oil at the end, the track was very slippery and very dangerous. The yellow hurt me in Toronto but helped me today."

Polesitter Tagliani led the field into Turn One, closely followed by his Player's teammate, Bertrand Godin. The racing behind them was fierce with Anthony Lazzaro moving from sixth to third in the opening lap. Barron passed his Lynx Racing teammate Memo Gidley for fourth and challenged Lazzaro for third before taking the spot on lap four.

< 163 >

Barron and Godin engaged in a heated battle that allowed Tagliani to extend his lead. Barron was able to pass Godin for second on the inside while entering Turn One on lap eight. From there Godin was plagued by brake and other mechanical problems that soon put him out of contention as one challenger after another got by. Barron, however, began to chase down the leader.

The first of three cautions occured on lap 11 for a crash by Jeret Schroeder, who became airborne and hit the wall hard after an altercation with Chuck West. Schroeder escaped with a sore neck and back.

On the restart, 11th -placed Cam Binder collected the tire wall in Turn Ten, and in an unrelated melee, David Cutler, George Frazier, Michael David and Mark Tague collected each other to bring the caution back out.

Tagliani maintained his lead on the lap 23 restart, but, Barbosa began to apply heavy pressure to Barron for second. Lazzaro and Kenny Wilden battled for fourth position, but Wilden was unable to continue the battle as his brakes began to fail. Gidley passed him on lap 38 as his brake woes continued.

Bob Thomas' car erupted in flames on lap 38 as he began to leak oil as he crossed the start-finish line. He put down a heavy oil trail between Turns Two and Three, giving Barbosa the opportunity he needed to pass Barron on the oil-soaked track.

The yellow flag flew for the final time on lap 39 and the timed race ended under caution. Tagliani led Barbosa and Barron to the checkered flag, with Lazzaro and Gidley following in fourth and fifth.

Tagliani took home the $20,000 winner's purse, $1,000 for the "KOOL Move of the Race" and $1,000 for the "Yokohama Now You've Got Control" award. Barbosa earned the $1,000 "KOOL Rookie Challenge" prize. Barron won the "MCI Fast Pace Award" for running the quickest laps of the race.

< 165 >

POLE POSITION
Alexandre Tagliani

RESULTS
Alexandre Tagliani
Joao Barbosa
Alex Barron
Anthony Lazzaro
Memo Gidley
Kenny Wilden
Chris Smith
Steve Knapp
Case Montgomery
Chuck West

| STANDINGS | POINTS |
|---|---|
| Alex Barron | 100 |
| Memo Gidley | 91 |
| Alexandre Tagliani | 88 |
| Bertrand Godin | 82 |
| Case Montgomery | 75 |
| Anthony Lazzaro | 74 |
| Joao Barbosa | 68 |
| Steve Knapp | 58 |
| Eric Lang | 47 |
| Tony Ave | 44 |

| C2 | POINTS |
|---|---|
| Joaquin DeSoto | 125 |
| James Irvin | 72 |
| Greg Harrington | 56 |
| Jimmy Pugliese | 46 |
| Frank Allers | 45 |

| KOOL Move of the Race | Alexandre Tagliani |
|---|---|
| KOOL Rookie Challenge | Joao Barbosa |
| Yokohama "Now You've Got Control" | Alexandre Tagliani |
| MCI Fast Pace Award | Alex Barron |

| PLAYER'S CHALLENGE | ROUND THREE |
|---|---|
| Memo Gidley | 45 |
| Alex Barron | 42 |
| Alexandre Tagliani | 38 |
| Bertrand Godin | 35 |
| Joao Barbosa | 28 |

< 167 >

# Rookie Barron goes for three

Lynx Racing Rookie Alex Barron traveled to the midwest to collect his third K⦻L /Toyota Atlantic Championship victory at the Mid-Ohio Sportscar Course, in Lexington, Ohio. Bertrand Godin finished a strong second, scoring his third podium appearance of 1997. Jeret Schroeder's third place effort was his highest finish of the season.

Polesitter Schroeder was immediately challenged following the F-1 style standing start, as Barron moved by him in Turn One. Equally competitive racing action followed behind the leaders as Chuck West had moved into seventh place from his 12th starting spot by the time the first yellow flag flew on lap14.

< 169 >

On the lap 19 restart, West drove hard into Turn Two to put the move on Joaquin DeSoto, but the two made contact, sending West firmly off course and into the tire barrier, ending his charge to the front.

Two additional incidents on the same lap brought out the yellow flag and slowed the field, with Barron maintaining his lead. This set up a two-lap dash to the checkered flag.

On the last lap of the event, Bertrand Godin challenged Schroeder for the second position, diving to the inside and making it stick in Turn Two. Schroeder stayed with it, but was unable to reclaim the spot and had to settle for third at the checkers.

Barron picked up this third winner's check of $20,000, and an additional $2,000 for the KOOL Rookie Challenge bonus and the MCI Fast Pace Award. Godin collected the second place trophy, along with the $1,000 "KOOL Move of the Race" and $1,000 "Yokohama Now You've Got Control" bonuses.

< 171 >

POLE POSITION
Jeret Schroeder

RESULTS
Alex Barron
Bertrand Godin
Jeret Schroeder
Memo Gidley
Steve Knapp
Joao Barbosa
Alexandre Tagliani
Anthony Lazzaro
Ted Sahley
Case Montgomery

| STANDINGS | POINTS |
|---|---|
| Alex Barron | 121 |
| Memo Gidley | 103 |
| Bertrand Godin | 98 |
| Alexandre Tagliani | 97 |
| Anthony Lazzaro | 82 |
| Case Montgomery | 81 |
| Joao Barbosa | 78 |
| Steve Knapp | 69 |
| Jeret Schroeder | 51 |
| Eric Lang | 48 |

| C2 | POINTS |
|---|---|
| Joaquin DeSoto | 142 |
| James Irvin | 86 |
| Howie Liebengood | 61 |
| Greg Harrington | 56 |
| Jimmy Pugliese | 46 |

Place : Mid-Ohio
Date : August 10, 1997
Round :
Track Length : 2.25 Mile
road course
Race Length : 25 laps

| | |
|---|---|
| KOOL Move of the Race | Bertrand Godin |
| KOOL Rookie Challenge | Alex Barron |
| Yokohama "Now You've Got Control" | Bertrand Godin |
| MCI Fast Pace Award | Alex Barron |

< 175 >

Place : Elkhart Lake
Date : August 17, 1997
Round : 10
Track Length : 4.048-mile road course
Race Length : 11 Laps

## Barron on a roll

Under gray skies and moderate rain at the 4.048-mile Road America track in Elkhart Lake, Wis., Lynx Racing's Alex Barron won his second straight, and the fourth KOOL /Toyota Atlantic Championship race of his rookie season. His flag-to-flag win in the rain helped him extend his lead in the point standings, with just two races remaining on the schedule.

Barron, who qualified third on the grid, seized the opportunity to take the lead with a superb standing start on the drenched track. Slipping with mere inches to spare between pole-sitter Chuck West and the wall, Barron was fully in command of the lead well before the first turn. Although second-place finisher Joao Barbosa was in his mirrors for the entire race, Barron was never seriously challenged.

"We made a major set up change just before we pushed the car to the grid and it worked out really well," said Barron. "The defining moment of my race was being able to move into the lead because I know that trying to run behind someone in weather like this makes it very difficult to move up. During the middle of the race, the track actually dried out just a little bit and we were all driving a little off-line to stay on the wet parts, but then the rain came back, and when it did, several cars spun off simultaneously and the race finished under yellow. I'd rather win under green, but this series is so competitive that you take your victories however they come."

Polesitter Chuck West stalled at the start of the race dropping him to 13th before the field rounded the first turn. Other drivers moved to the back just as quickly as the field coped with impaired vision and a rain soaked racing line.

< 177 >

Wisconsin native Steve Knapp used his "home-field advantage" to pass Anthony Lazzaro for third position on lap 2, as Bertrand Godin passed Memo Gidley for fourth. Lazzaro crossed the start-finish line for the second time in sixth place.

"I knew the track was pretty slippery on the race line in the wet," said West, "so I was driving off-line pretty much all the way around."

Lap three saw a full course caution as vehicles went spinning off course all around the circuit. Several cars visited the gravel traps and a blower had to be brought on track to clear the mess before the race could return to green. As the field restarted on lap eight, Barron, Barbosa, Knapp, Godin and Gidley led Lazzaro, now in sixth. At the green, Barron held off the advances of Barbosa and it was follow-the-leader until Chuck West went off in turn twelve and hit the wall, while Lazzaro got into the gravel in Turn Three.

Again, the caution flag flew and on Lap 11 the race ended under yellow due to time constraints.

The $20,000 prize for first place went to Barron, who also collected the $1,000 KOOL Rookie Challenge bonus along with the MCI Fast Pace Award. Barbosa accepted the second place trophy followed by Knapp in third. Although he did not appear on the podium, Godin collected the $1,000 "KOOL Move of the Race" and $1,000 "Yokohama Now You've Got Control" awards, for moving from his 12th place starting position to a fourth place finish under extremely difficult racing conditions.

< 179 >

## POLE POSITION
Chuck West

## RESULTS
Alex Barron
Joao Barbosa
Steve Knapp
Bertrand Godin
Memo Gidley
Alexandre Tagliani
Tony Ave
Jeret Schroeder
Case Montgomery
Kenny Wilden

| STANDINGS | POINTS |
|---|---|
| Alex Barron | 142 |
| Memo Gidley | 114 |
| Bertrand Godin | 110 |
| Alexandre Tagliani | 107 |
| Joao Barbosa | 94 |
| Case Montgomery | 88 |
| Steve Knapp | 83 |
| Anthony Lazzaro | 82 |
| Jeret Schroeder | 59 |
| Tony Ave | 53 |

| C2 | POINTS |
|---|---|
| Joaquin DeSoto | 159 |
| James Irvin | 86 |
| Howie Liebengood | 81 |
| Greg Harrington | 56 |
| Jimmy Pugliese | 46 |

Place : Elkhart Lake
Date : August 17, 1997
Round : 10
Track Length : 4.048-mile
road course
Race Length : 11 Laps

| | |
|---|---|
| KOOL Move of the Race | Bertrand Godin |
| KOOL Rookie Challenge | Alex Barron |
| Yokohama "Now You've Got Control" | Bertrand Godin |
| MCI Fast Pace Award | Alex Barron |

< 181 >

Place : Vancouver
Date : August 30, 1997
Round : 11
Track Length : 1.703-mile street course
Race Length : 38 laps

## Gidley goes for two

Lynx Racing driver Memo Gidley went wire-to-wire to capture his second KOOL/Toyota Atlantic Championship victory of the season on the streets around Vancouver's Concord Pacific Place. Gidley's teammate and points leader, Alex Barron, finished third behind Steve Knapp, completing the season's second all-rookie podium. Mathematically speaking, the two Lynx Racing teammates were now the only drivers who could capture the Atlantic championship.

Gidley, who set a new track record in qualifying, toured the ten-turn street circuit at an average speed of 64.714 mph and crossed the finish line 1.731-seconds ahead of Knapp.

"I feel like I graduated from school today," said Gidley. "I've been learning like mad all season and now it's all coming together. My car was working well, but so were the other two guys, so I didn't have one instant to relax. The Lynx team gave me a great car and Paul Hasselgren gave me a great engine. I'm happy to go to the final race knowing that either Alex or I will be the champion."

Gidley took the green light on the Atlantic standing start and led the field through Turn One. Meanwhile, Michael David was unable to pull away from the grid due to transmission troubles and was struck from behind by Jeret Schroeder. In a distant chain reaction, Anthony Lazzaro rear-ended Joao Barbosa, forcing that car to the pits with suspension damage. The melee brought out a red flag as workers scrambled to clean up the mess.

Officials decided on a rolling start, and Gidley charged into the lead with Knapp and Barron in hot pursuit. Bill Tichenor brought out the first caution with a spin in Turn Seven.

< 183 >

When racing resumed on lap 11, Gidley pulled safely away from Knapp and Barron, who engaged in a fierce battle for second. Meanwhile Montgomery made a daring inside pass on fifth-placed Lazzaro. They banged wheels, with Montgomery squeezing by to take the position.

While the top three pulled away unchallenged, Kenny Wilden got by Lazzaro and gave Montgomery all the pressure he could stand. The multi-lap battle would eventualy go to the checkered, with Montgomery retaining fourth place, while the top three finished in their battle order of Gidley, Knapp and Barron.

If Barron could have secured the spot he would have assured himself of the Atlantic championship, succeeding CART driver Patrick Carpentier, who won the title last year for Lynx Racing. Yet, Knapp, having his best weekend of the season after starting on the outside pole, aggressively and successfully defended his position from Barron's challenges.

"My car was really good, but it's hard to pass here and I couldn't seem to get by," said Barron. "I'm pretty pleased with what happened. We'll go into Laguna like it's just another race and go for it. The team gave me a great car but I decided that if I couldn't get by safely, I'd settle for third which goes against my grain, but that's what had to be done."

Gidley took home the $20,000 check for his first place finish and earned the $1,000 KOOL Rookie Challenge award. Case Montgomery did not finish on the podium, but picked up $1,000 for the "KOOL Move of the Race" and $1,000 for the "Yokohama Now You've Got Control" bonuses, while Alex Barron scored the MCI Fast Pace Award.

< 185 >

## POLE POSITION
Memo Gidley

## RESULTS
Memo Gidley
Steve Knapp
Alex Barron
Case Montgomery
Kenny Wilden
Anthony Lazzaro
Bertrand Godin
Eric Lang
Cam Binder
John Rutherford

| STANDINGS | POINTS |
|---|---|
| Alex Barron | 156 |
| Memo Gidley | 136 |
| Bertrand Godin | 119 |
| Alexandre Tagliani | 109 |
| Case Montgomery | 100 |
| Steve Knapp | 99 |
| Joao Barbosa | 94 |
| Anthony Lazzaro | 92 |
| Jeret Schroeder | 59 |
| Eric Lang | 56 |

| C2 | POINTS |
|---|---|
| Joaquin DeSoto | 159 |
| James Irvin | 86 |
| Howie Liebengood | 81 |
| Frank Allers | 66 |
| Jimmy Pugliese | |

Place : Vancouver
Date : August 30, 1997
Round : 11
Track Length : 1.703 mile street course
Race Length : 36 laps

| | |
|---|---|
| KOOL Move of the Race | Case Montgomery |
| KOOL Rookie Challenge | Memo Gidley |
| Yokohama "Now You've Got Control" | Case Montgomery |
| MCI Fast Pace Award | Alex Barron |

## PLAYER'S CHALLENGE
## FINAL STANDINGS ROUND FOUR
Memo Gidley
Alex Barron
Bertrand Godin
Alexandre Tagliani
Case Montgomery

< 187 >

Place : Laguna Seca
Date : September 6, 1997
Round : 12
Track Length : 2.238-mile road course
Race Length : 28 laps

## Barron champion with victory

"The champion shall not be denied" was the phrase of the day for newly crowned KOOL/Toyota Atlantic Championship title winner Alex Barron. Barron secured the championship by capturing the pole on the last lap of final qualifying with a record setting speed of 102.302 mph. He eclipsed the record set by teammate Memo Gidley the day before. With the one point bonus he earned for the pole, Barron assured himself the title.

Barron survived a first lap incident with third place starter Anthony Lazzaro and a self-induced mid-race spin to prevail over David Pook by 5.853 seconds in the 28-lap race.

On the start Lazzaro drove inside of Barron and Gidley entering Turn One. Barron and Lazzaro touched, sending Lazzaro's car airborne. Lazzaro limped to the pits and retired, while Barron never missed a beat and continued with Gidley hot on his heels.

"I got a good start," said Lazzaro. "Alex (Barron) picked up on the line. I had already chosen the inside and when I got up there, he started moving over and we made contact. I think he realized he didn't get a good start and wanted to move over to defend his position and I was there."

Gidley took advantage of traffic on lap 14 to overtake his Lynx Racing teammate, whose car was beginning to show some signs that the earlier contact may have exacted some damage after all.

"Every time I would let off the gas in third, the gear would come out and it would pop into neutral," Barron said. "The car would free-wheel, and then it would start to slide."

Barron then spun exiting turn 11 on lap 15, allowing Gidley to extend a significant lead. Gidley appeared to be on his way to a second consecutive victory until his gearbox failed, giving the lead back to Barron on lap 21.

< 189 >

With Barron back in the lead by a significant eight second margin, Pook tried valiantly to reel him in, already having charged from sixth to second. Pook, suffering without a car radio, gave it all he could, triming nearly four seconds off Barron's cushion, but ran out of laps and had to settle for second.

"It's a good way to end the year," said Pook. "It could only have been one better. But after some frustrating times this year, it is nice to go out on a good note."

Alexandre Tagliani and Michael David battled behind the leaders. David, who had moved quickly from his eleventh starting position, waged a fierce fight with Tagliani. The two drivers traded positions several times before Tagliani nailed down third behind Barron and Pook on lap 26. David finished fourth, followed by Jeret Schroeder.

"It was a pretty exciting race with a lot going on," said Barron. "Anthony Lazzaro ran into the side of me at the start and after that the steering was a little crooked, but the car handled fine. Then a few laps into the race my transmission started jumping out of third (gear) and I had to drive some of the turns with one hand. That was why I spun in Turn 11, but I didn't lose a place. I'm sorry my teammate Memo had mechanical problems because we were having a great race. I'm very happy for both myself and Lynx Racing to end the season with a win."

Barron collected the $20,000 winner's prize for the fifth time in 1997. He also earned the $1,000 KOOL Rookie Challenge award and the $1,000 MCI Fast Pace Award. David accepted the "KOOL Move of the Race" and "Yokohama Now You've Got Control" awards, adding $2,000 to his winnings.

< 191 >

## POLE POSITION
Alex Barron

## RESULTS
Alex Barron
David Pook
Alexandre Tagliani
Michael David
Jeret Schroeder
Kenny Wilden
Cam Binder
Eric Lang
Chuck West
Ted Sahley

| STANDINGS | POINTS |
|---|---|
| Alex Barron | 178 |
| Memo Gidley | 136 |
| Alexandre Tagliani | 123 |
| Bertrand Godin | 121 |
| Case Montgomery | 100 |
| Steve Knapp | 99 |
| Joao Barbosa | 94 |
| Anthony Lazzaro | 92 |
| Jeret Schroeder | 70 |
| Eric Lang | 64 |

| C2 | POINTS |
|---|---|
| Joaquin DeSoto | 159 |
| James Irvin | 86 |
| Howie Liebengood | 81 |
| Frank Allers | 66 |
| Jimmy Pugliese | 62 |

| | |
|---|---|
| KOOL Move of the Race | Michael David |
| KOOL Rookie Challenge | Alex Barron |
| Yokohama "Now You've Got Control" | Michael David |
| MCI Fast Pace Award | Alex Barron |

< 193 >

## 1997 KOOL/Toyota Atlantic Championship FINAL Standings

| | Driver | Sponsors | Starts | Points |
|---|---|---|---|---|
| 1. | Alex Barron | Lynx Racing / Victory Circle Racing / Red Line Oil | 12 | 178 |
| 2. | Memo Gidley | Lynx Racing | 12 | 136 |
| 3. | Alexandre Tagliani | Player's Forsythe Racing Team - Indeck | 11 | 123 |
| 4. | Bertrand Godin | Player's Forsythe Racing Team - Indeck | 12 | 121 |
| 5. | Case Montgomery | Binder Racing - Microsoft / Wall Data / Tandem / Compaq | 12 | 100 |
| 6. | Steve Knapp | P-1 Racing - NTN Bearings / Miller Milling | 11 | 99 |
| 7. | Joao Barbosa | RDS Motorsport / Agip - Toyota Portugal / Caetano Buses | 12 | 94 |
| 8. | Anthony Lazzaro. | Phillips Motorsports - Platinum Sound / BG Products / Budget | 12 | 92 |
| 9. | Jeret Schroeder | P.P.I. - MCI Racing | 12 | 70 |
| 10. | Eric Lang | D & L Racing - L.C.I. International | 12 | 64 |
| 11. | David Pook | B.D.J.S. - HYPE Energy Drink / Budweiser | 10 | 59 |
| 12. | Kenny Wilden | P-1 Racing - TrizecHahn / Slick 50 | 12 | 55 |
| 13. | Tony Ave | Olsson Engineering - Fisher Dynamics / Schuler Design | 8 | 53 |
| 14. | Chuck West | World Speed Motorsports - Red Line Oil | 11 | 46 |
| 15. | Bill Auberlen | B.D.J.S. | 4 | 38 |
| 16. | Cam Binder | Binder Racing - Western Avionics / Kenn Borek Air Ltd. | 12 | 38 |
| 17. | Michael David | PDR Enterprises - Water Joe / David Engineering & Mfg. | 11 | 30 |
| 18. | Ted Sahley | Sahley Racing Enterprises - Comfort Inn Surety Title / Pinnacle Financial / Climaco & Climaco L.P.A. | 12 | 23 |
| 19. | Robert Sollenskog | BRS Motorsports - Earl's Performance Products / Graphics in Motion | 6 | 18 |
| 20. | Mark Tague | World Speed Motorsports - Altec / Liaison Software Co. | 11 | 17 |
| 21. | David Cutler | Binder Racing - Microsoft / Wall Data / Tandem / Compaq | 12 | 13 |
| 22. | Joe Sposato | Sposato Motor Racing - Scott Air Pak | 6 | 13 |
| 23. | Chris Smith | P.P.I. - MCI Racing / Earl's Performance Products | 6 | 11 |
| 24. | Leo Parente | Phillips Motorsports | 6 | 9 |
| 25. | David Rutledge | B.D.J.S. - Fleming Financial / Keg Caesar's | 3 | 8 |
| 26. | Frank Allers | Johnston Engineering / Keen Engineering | 4 | 8 |
| 27. | Charles Nearburg | NRC Marketing / Nearburg Expl / Niederhoffer-Henkel | 1 | 8 |
| 28. | Stuart Crow | B.D.J.S. | 2 | 7 |
| 29. | John Rutherford | Mike Shank Racing - Pennzoil | 3 | 6 |
| 30. | Joaquin DeSoto | Weld Motorports - Canvas by Deneba Software | 9 | 5 |
| 31. | Steve Forrer | Steve Forrer Racing - Forrer Supply | 3 | 4 |

## 1997 KOOL/Toyota Atlantic Championship FINAL Standings

|     | Driver | Sponsors | Starts | Points |
|-----|--------|----------|--------|--------|
| 32. | Peter MacLeod | Team Medlin Racing - Evergreen Aviation | 1 | 4 |
| 33. | Carol Soucy | Dominic Scalzo Racing - Shell Canada / Eurocopter Canada / Heli-Excel | 3 | 3 |
| 34. | Sergei Szortyka | J & J Racing - Quaker Maid Meats / The Philly Steak / Mama Lucia Meatballs Philly Gourmet | 6 | 2 |
| 35. | Ian Bland | Kaditcha Racing - Japan Tonga | 3 | 2 |
| 36. | Paet Hidalgo | Binder Racing - America Online / Rennspeed | 2 | 1 |
| 37. | Stephane Roy | Hammerhead Racing / Ben Gay / Musique Plus/ Mix96 / Gatortade | 3 | 1 |
| 38. | Mattias Andersson | BRS Motorsports / I.F.S. / Channel 5 | 1 | 1 |
| 39. | Bob Siska | R.J.S. Motorsports | 6 | – |
| 40. | John Brooks | BBGP / Drive 4 Life Racing / Port-a-Cool | 8 | – |
| 41. | Jimmy Pugliese | Hunter-Smith Pugliese Motorsports - Sierra / Pennzoil / Papyrus Design Group FRAM | 4 | – |
| 42. | Howie Liebengood | CompPrep - National Campaign to Stop Violence | 5 | – |
| 43. | James Irvin | E. Milner Irvin / Riverside Motorsports | 5 | – |
| 44. | George Frazier | Arcadia Motorsports Ltd. | 5 | – |
| 45. | Scott Wood | Phillips Motorsports - Wood Energy Corp. | 3 | – |
| 46. | Buddy Brundo | Hammerhead Racing / Conway Recording Studios / Eibach Springs | 3 | – |
| 47. | Roy Haryanto | Binder Racing - Gudnang Garam | 1 | – |
| 48. | Dave Hall | Dave Hall Racing - H.O.F. | 1 | – |
| 49. | Mike Sauce | Mike Sauce Motorsports / Top Dawg | 1 | – |
| 50. | Bob McGregor | McGregor Racing - Britco Structures | 1 | – |
| 51. | Dan Vosloo | Danvo Racing / Danvo Machining | 2 | – |
| 52. | Jim Ward | Bertil's Racing Engines - Travis Development Co. | 1 | – |
| 53. | Michael Simpson | Simpson Motorsports - Maaco Autobody / Pik A Part | 3 | – |
| 54. | Brian Dunkel | Cary Marathon Inc. | 2 | – |
| 55. | Kevin Cogan | Cogan Motorsports | 3 | – |
| 56. | Greg Harrington | Greg Harrington Racing - Valvoline / Performance Friction | 4 | – |
| 57. | Bob Thomas | Different Drummer Racing - Terry Machine Co. / Trenton Forging | 4 | – |
| 58. | Bill Tichenor | World Speed Motorsports - Heftel Broadcasting / Comp USA | 3 | – |
| 59. | Brian French | French Racing - Motorsports Enterprises | 1 | – |
| 60. | Brian Battaglia | Phillips Motorsports - ADA Custom Masonry | 1 | – |
| 61. | Martin Roy | LeVolant Motorsports | 1 | – |
| 62. | Yoichi Akase | Phillips Motorsports - Autopiar Country | 1 | – |
| 63. | M. Camirand | Cogan Motorsports | 1 | – |
| 64. | Marcelo Gaffoglio | TGF Metalcraft / The Tonight Show | 2 | – |

< 195 >

| | | |
|---|---|---|
| KTAC Champion & KOOL Series Cup | Alex Barron | Lynx Racing / Victory Circle |
| KOOL Rookie Challenge | Alex Barron | Lynx Racing / Victory Circle |
| Gilles Villeneuve Award | Jeret Schroeder | PPI-MCI Racing |
| Snap-On Top Wrench | Dave Spencer | P-1 Racing |
| Team Owner of the Year | Brian Robertson | BDJS |
| Rising Star Award | Joao Barbosa | RDS Motorsports |
| Michael Rosen Memorial Trophy | Michael David | PDR Enterprises |
| TRD Engine Builder of the Year | Paul Hasselgren | Hasselgren Racing |
| Crew Chief of the Year | Rick Cameron | Lynx Racing |
| Engineer of the Year | Jim Griffith | Lynx Racing |
| Jovy Marcelo Sportsmanship Award | Case Montgomery | Binder Racing |
| C2 Championship Award | Joaquin DeSoto | Weld Motorsports |
| KOOL Racing Challenge | Alexandre Tagliani | Player's Forsythe Racing |

## Player's Challenge Championship Awards

| | | |
|---|---|---|
| 1st | Memo Gidley | Lynx Racing |
| 2nd | Alex Barron | Lynx Racing / Victory Circle |
| 3rd | Bertrand Godin | Player's Forsythe Racing |

## Top Canadian Finishers

| | | |
|---|---|---|
| 1st | Bertrand Godin | Player's Forsythe Racing |
| 2nd | Alexandre Tagliani | Player's Forsythe Racing |
| 3rd | Kenny Wilden | P-1 Racing |

| | |
|---|---|
| Player's Pit Stop Competition Masters | Lynx Racing |

## KOOL/Toyota Atlantic Championship

| | | |
|---|---|---|
| 1st | Alex Barron ( R ) | Lynx Racing / Victory Circle |
| 2nd | Memo Gidley ( R ) | Lynx Racing |
| 3rd | Alexandre Tagliani | Player's Forsythe Racing |
| 4th | Bertrand Godin ( R ) | Player's Forsythe Racing |
| 5th | Case Montgomery | Binder Racing |
| 6th | Steve Knapp ( R ) | P-1 Racing |
| 7th | Joao Barbosa ( R ) | RDS Motorsports |
| 8th | Anthony Lazzaro | Phillips Motorsports |
| 9th | Jeret Schroeder | PPI-MCI Racing |
| 10th | Eric Lang | D & L Racing |

## 1997 KOOL/Toyota Atlantic Awards Banquet - Sun, Sept. 7, 1997 - Monterey, Calif.
### Rookie Alex Barron Honored as 1997 KOOL /Toyota Atlantic Champion

Following a climactic weekend of racing that saw the battle for the 1997 KOOL/Toyota Atlantic Championship title go down to the last qualifying session, the Atlantic drivers, teams, owners, officials, sponsors, friends and families gathered at the Hyatt Regency Monterey to celebrate a highly competitive season and honor the victors at the 24th Annual Awards Banquet. Atlantic series' own, Greg Creamer shared Master of Ceremonies duties with Bob Varsha of ABC Sports, and the duo kept the evening moving with exciting video high-lights during the trophy & award presentations.

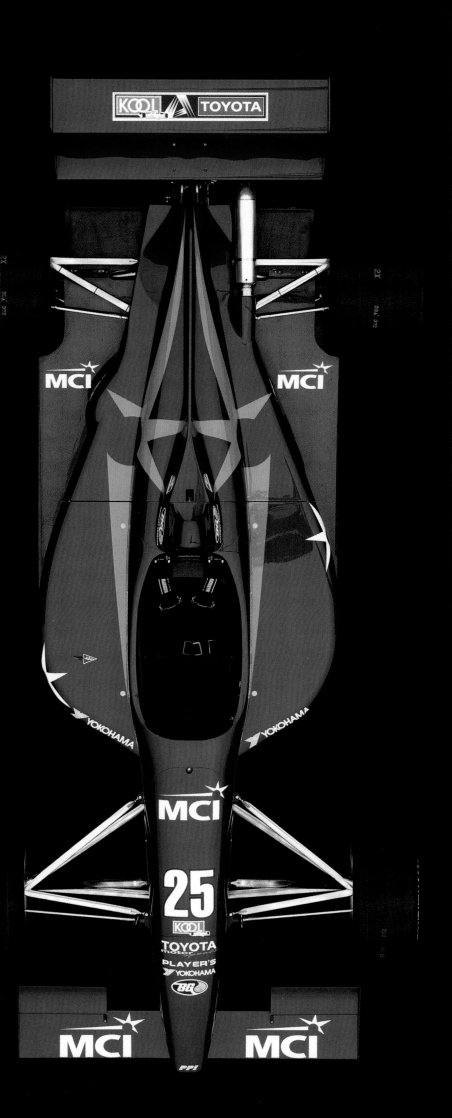

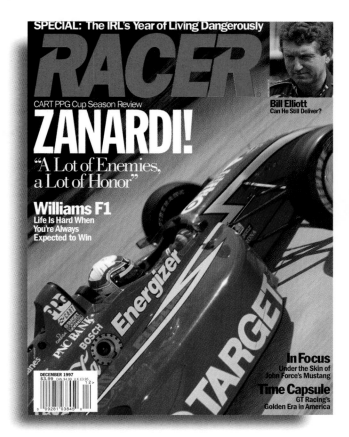

First of all I must congratulate Vicki, and all the past and present supporters and champions of the Atlantic Series, for 25 years of outstanding competition!

I would also like to congratulate 1997 KOOL/Toyota Atlantic Champion, Alex Barron, and all of the winners in the 1997 Atlantic Championship. KOOL is a proud co-title sponsor of this exciting series, and I was delighted with the level of competition for our initiatives which proved so popular this year.

The 'KOOL Rookie of the Year Challenge' was awarded to the champ, Alex Barron – a fitting testament to his outstanding performance in just his rookie season! But it was a closely fought contest, and I am delighted to be able to say that we will be continuing the challenges into next season.

For Alexandre Tagliani, as the 'KOOL Racing Challenge' winner who pocketed $10,000 and our special Zurini trophy, I also extend my congratulations. Also, with such an extremely competitive field, the 'KOOL Move of the Race' was one of the most difficult to determine, with a different winner nearly every race!

The Atlantic Championship has long been recognized as a training ground for up-and-coming open wheel stars. As this book beautifully illustrates, the Atlantic roster is a who's-who of stars, with such names as Rahal, Sullivan, Andretti and the Villeneuves, just to name a few. For us, the chance to be involved in such a competitive series with such talented drivers is important. These are the men who will go on to drive in the most prestigious championships in the world, and it is vital that they receive all the help and training that they need at this level.

KOOL will be back on board for '98 and I am looking forward to another exciting and closely-fought championship. I wish Vicki and Jerry all the best as we usher in the next 25 years of future champions.

Best Regards,

*Bert Kremer*

Bert Kremer
Sponsorship Manager
Brown & Williamson Tobacco

< 201 >

## One make for the future

The Silver Anniversary season of the KⓄL/Toyota Atlantic Championship marks a departure of sorts, as the series begins phasing in a one-make chassis to complement its specified engine and tire components. This is not, however, as radical a philosophical change as it might at first seem, since at regular intervals throughout its history Atlantic has been prone to domination by a single marque.

Only in its earliest years did the formula feature a true wide-open battle among a variety of different chassis, as cars built by English constructors Lotus, Lola, March and Chevron shared the successes of those first two championship seasons. Based on Gilles Villeneuve's domination of the series in 1976 and '77, March took control of the chassis sweepstakes. March, Chevron and newcomer Ralt all scored victories during the '78 season with Ralt and March then dividing the spoils fairly equally between them until Ralt brought out its RT-4, the formula's first ground-effects car, in 1980.

Beginning with Kevin Cogan's victory in the 1981 season finale in Montreal, Ralt's RT-4 won an unprecedented 76 consecutive professional Atlantic races over the course of the next six seasons, until its streak was snapped and its reign succeeded by the American-built Swift DB-4. The RT-4 benefited not only from a long tenure as the chassis of choice, but also from the fact that its lifetime coincided with flourishing series on both coasts that generated yearly race counts running as high as 21.

Apart from a brief foray into the formula by Reynard in the early '90s, Swift held sway until Ralt returned with its RT40 midway through the '92 season. Ralts won all but one race in each of '93 and '94. With the 40, and its next generation RT41, Ron Tauranac's company re-established its hold on Atlantic, sweeping every race of the next three seasons. Ralts have won more than half of the pro Atlantic races ever held. Now, for 1998, comes the Swift 008.a, designed by Roman Slobodynskyj with assistance from David Bruns and Mark Handford. Like the RT-4, DB-4 and RT40 before it, the 008.a brings Atlantic into step with the current state of modern racing car art. It will compete for the first time in 1998, and be phased in over the next two seasons, becoming the only eligible chassis at the turn of the century.

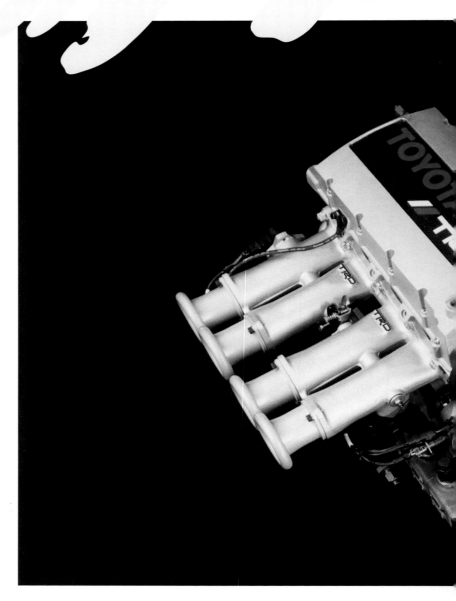

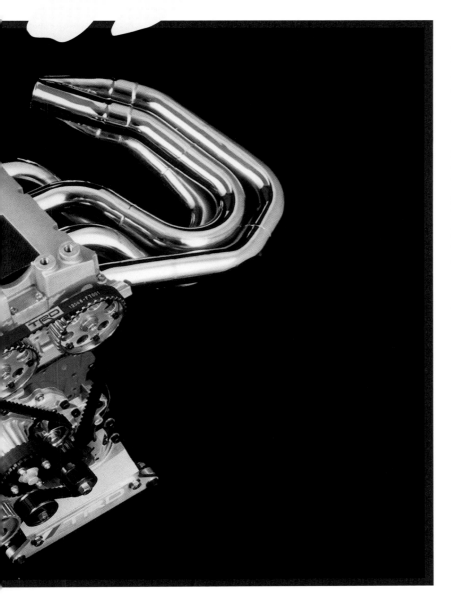

The 008.a is built to Swift's usual high standards of quality and features a raised-nose carbon-fiber monocoque powered by a revised version of Toyota's 4A-GE engine that drives through a 5-speed sequentially shifted Hewland gearbox. The latest development of the 240hp Toyota engine includes an upgraded electronic engine management system incorporating a shift-without-lift feature and improved data-diagnostic capability. The 008.a carries its engine lower in the chassis thanks to a redesigned oil sump system, and improves the overall stiffness of the chassis with a new cast magnesium cam cover. It has also been designed to accommodate the introduction of a new 15-inch Yokohama radial as the series' spec tire. Driver safety has been a primary consideration all through the design and build process-the car's nosebox meets Formula 3000 crash standards-and cockpit dimensions have been eased so that drivers of more average heights and weights can fit comfortably into the car.

The new Swift 008.A-Toyota sells for $91,500 and is being distributed by Carl Haas Auto Imports in Lincolnshire, Ill.

| | Constructor | Wins |
|---|---|---|
| 1. | Ralt | 155 |
| 2. | Swift | 81 |
| 3. | March | 41 |
| 4. | Lola | 9 |
| 5. | Chevron | 8 |
| | Reynard | 8 |
| 7. | Lotus | 3 |

While the above list shows overall wins by each constructor in Atlantic history, the chart below notes the dominant years of the series' most successful chassis models, calculates their winning percentages during the time span between their first and last victories and shows the longest win streak for each.

| Chassis | Winning Years | Races | Wins | Pctg. | Consec. |
|---|---|---|---|---|---|
| Ralt RT40-41[*] | '93-'97 | 67 | 61 | .910 | 37 |
| March 76B-77B | '76-'77 | 21 | 19 | .905 | 9 |
| Ralt RT-4 | '80-'87 | 100 | 84 | .840 | 76 |
| Swift DB-4 | '87-'94 | 116 | 81 | .698 | 34 |

[*]still active

< 203 >

## Swift 008.a Toyota Atlantic

### Specifications

| | |
|---|---|
| *Overall Length* | 167 in (4241.8mm) |
| *Wheelbase* | 104 in. (2641.6mm) |
| *Track*   Front: | 66 in.    (1676.4 mm) |
|             Rear: | 61in.     (1549.4 mm) |
| *Weight* | 550 kg. With driver |
| *Suspension* | Double wishbone, front and rear, pushrod actuated |
| *Chassis Construction* | Carbon fiber monocoque with Indy car type ground effect tunnels |
| *Wheels* | BBS, forged aluminum |
|   Front: | 15 in. diameter x 10 in. wide |
|   Rear: | 15 in. diameter x 14 in. wide |
| *Tires* | Yokohama radial ply tires |
| *Gearbox* | Hewland, 5-speed, sequential, "no-lift" shift with reverse |
| *Instrumentation* | Pi System 2 |
| *Brakes* | Brembo, calipers and discs |
| *Engine* | TRD (Toyota Racing Development) modified Toyota 4AGE, four cylinder, four valves per cylinder, double overhead cam |
|   *Displacement:* | 1.6 liter |
|   *Compression Ratio:* | 13:1 |
|   *Maximum Horsepower:* | 240 hp @ 9500 rpm |
|   *Maximum Torque:* | 130 ft./lb. |
|   *Induction System:* | TRD electronic fuel injection |
| *Performance* | |
|   *Top Speed:* | 150+ mph |
|   *Acceleration:* | 0-60 mph - approx. 4 sec. |

< 205 >

## Vicki O'Connor
### Looking ahead, the next 25 years:

As I look ahead at the next 25 years of the Atlantic series, I hope that Atlantic will remained positioned as one of the top driver development series in the world, and will continue to graduate drivers to the highest echelon of the sport. That's the main role that we play, and that will never change.

Today, Atlantic is in excellent health. In 1997 we had 45 cars at Long Beach, and we averaged 32 cars per race. We are racing on the weekends we want with the CART series, and we continue to race at the Montreal Grand Prix, which is very prestigious. Thus, we are strongly positioned. Over the past 25 years, the series has shown that a driver can go from Atlantic to Indy cars and be successful. Most recently we've graduated Jimmy Vasser, Jacques Villeneuve, Richie Hearn, Patrick Carpentier, and now Alex Barron. The formula is working like never before.

Despite this success, we can not rest on our laurels. Building for the future is an ongoing process, and we face that challenge every day. It is our responsibility to make sure we're doing an excellent job for our sponsors and our teams. We are always coming up with new ideas, new ways to improve the series, and to improve its exposure and popularity with sports fans everywhere. If we're still here in 25 years, we will have done a good job.

In August of 1996 I sold the Atlantic series to Jerry Forsythe. The series had grown to where we had a lot of people making their living from it. Many people depended on me, and there wasn't anyone to take over. That worried me. I wanted to see Atlantic in an organization where, if the day came that I no longer wanted to run it or if something happened, the series would be healthy and would have a home. I'd known Jerry for years and he had always been a firm supporter of Atlantic, so we made a deal. It was the right thing to do. Atlantic needed to be secure within a larger organization, and I'm confident that under Jerry's stewardship it will prosper well into the next millennium. That is my gift.

< 207 >

## CAREER VICTORIES 1974 TO 1997

| 1. | Mark Dismore | 15 | | Russell Spence | 3 |
|---|---|---|---|---|---|
| 2. | Claude Bourbonnais | 13 | | Brian Till | 3 |
| | Gilles Villeneuve | 13 (1) | 42. | Michael Angus | 2 |
| 3. | Patrick Carpentier | 12 | | Geoff Brabham | 2 |
| 4. | David Empringham | 11 | | Tim Coconis | 2 |
| 5. | Dan Marvin | 10 | | Bob Earl | 2 |
| | Jacques Villeneuve° | 10 | | Elliot Forbes-Robinson | 2 |
| 8. | Dean Hall | 9 | | Memo Gidley | 2 |
| 9. | Bill Brack | 8 (2) | | Bertrand Godin | 2 |
| | Jimmy Vasser | 8 | | Scott Harrington | 2 |
| | Jeff Wood | 8 | | Anthony Lazzaro | 2 |
| 12. | Jocko Cunningham | 7 | | Jovy Marcelo | 2 |
| | Calvin Fish | 7 | | Case Montgomery | 2 |
| | Richie Hearn | 7 | | Hubert Phipps | 2 |
| 15. | Scott Goodyear | 6 | | Roberto Quintanilla | 2 |
| | Tom Klausler | 6 (3) | | Freddy Rhemrev | 2 |
| | Johnny O'Connell | 6 | | Rogelio Rodriguez | 2 |
| 18. | Alex Barron | 5 | | Bertil Roos | 2 |
| | Howdy Holmes | 5 | | Alexandre Tagliani | 2 |
| | Hiro Matsushita | 5 | | John Tanner | 2 |
| | Roberto Moreno | 5 | | Mitch Theiman | 2 |
| | Steve Shelton | 5 | 61. | Tony Ave | 1 |
| | Colin Trueman | 5 | | Chris Bender | 1 |
| | Jacques Villeneuve°° | 5 | | Rod Bennett | 1 (1) |
| 25. | Price Cobb | 4 (1) | | Vittorio Brambilla | 1 |
| | Kevin Cogan | 4 | | David Diem | 1 |
| | Ted Prappas | 4 | | Josele Garza | 1 |
| | Keke Rosberg | 4 | | Rod Granberry | 1 |
| | R.K. Smith | 4 (1) | | Harald Huysman | 1 |
| 30. | Michael Andretti | 3 | | Riley Hopkins | 1 |
| | John David Briggs | 3 | | Davy Jones | 1 |
| | Stuart Crow | 3 | | Allen Lader | 1 |
| | Whitney Ganz | 3 | | Marty Loft | 1 |
| | Tom Gloy | 3 | | Dave McMillan | 1 |
| | Michael Greenfield | 3 | | Mark Moore | 1 |
| | Tom Phillips | 3 | | Bill O'Connor | 1 |
| | Bobby Rahal | 3 | | Stephane Proulx | 1 |
| | Greg Ray | 3 | | Steve Saleen | 1 |
| | Trevor Seibert | 3 (2) | 79. | Joe Sposato | 1 |
| | Chris Smith | 3 | | | |

( ) non-championship wins included in total ° brother of Gilles Villeneuve °° son of Gilles Villeneuve

| YEAR | CHAMPION | CHASSIS | POINTS | WINS |
|---|---|---|---|---|
| 1997 | Alex Barron (R) | Ralt RT-41 | 178 | 5 |
| 1996 | Patrick Carpentier | Ralt RT-41 | 239 | 9 |
| 1995 | Richie Hearn | Ralt RT-41 | 201 | 3 |
| 1994 | David Empringham | Ralt RT-41 | 162 | 2 |
| 1993 | David Empringham | Ralt RT-41 | 195 | 1 |
| 1992 | Chris Smith | Swift DB-4 | 150 | 3 |
| 1991 | Jovy Marcelo | Swift DB-4 | 157 | 2 |
| 1990-A | Brian Till | Swift DB-4 | 149 | 3 |
| 1990-P | Mark Dismore | Swift DB-4 | 154 | 7 |
| 1989-A | Jocko Cunningham | Swift DB-4 | 184 | 4 |
| 1989-P | Hiro Matsushita | Swift DB-4 | 141 | 4 |
| 1988-A | Steve Shelton | Swift DB-4 | 137 | 3 |
| 1988-P | Dean Hall | Swift DB-4 | 160 | 5 |
| 1987-A | Calvin Fish | Ralt RT-4 | 149 | 3 |
| 1987-P | Johnny O'Connell | Ralt RT-4 | 141 | 4 |
| 1986-A | Scott Goodyear | Ralt RT-4 | 139 | 5 |
| 1986-P | Ted Prappas | Ralt RT-4 | 113 | 4 |
| 1985-A | Michael Angus | Ralt RT-4 | 102 | 1 |
| 1985-P | Jeff Wood | Ralt RT-4 | 144 | 4 |
| 1984 | Dan Marvin | Ralt RT-4 | 116 | 5 |
| 1983 | Michael Andretti | Ralt RT-4 | 188 | 3 |
| 1982 | Dave McMillan | Ralt RT-4 | 120 | 1 |
| 1981 | Jacques Villeneuve | March 81A | 166 | 4 |
| 1980 | Jacques Villeneuve | March 80A | 178 | 4 |
| 1979 | Tom Gloy | Ralt RT-1 | 208 | 1 |
| 1978 | Howdy Holmes | March 78B | 131 | 2 |
| 1977 | Gilles Villeneuve | March 77B | 114 | 3 |
| 1976-CASC | Gilles Villeneuve | March 76B | 120 | 5 |
| 1976-IMSA | Gilles Villeneuve | March 76B | 80 | 4 |
| 1975 | Bill Brack | Chevron B29 | 112 | 1 |
| 1974 | Bill Brack | Lotus 59/69 | 128 | 4 |

*A = Atlantic Division    P = Pacific Division*

**CHASSIS VICTORIES**

| | | | |
|---|---|---|---|
| Ralt | 154 | Chevron | 8 (2) |
| Swift | 82 (3) | Lola | 8 (3) |
| March | 42 (3) | Reynard | 8 |
| | | Lotus | 2 |

( ) non-championship wins included in total

< 209 >

## INDIVIDUAL DRIVER RECORDS
## THROUGH 1997 SEASON

most career races: Joe Sposato, *105*
most career victories: Mark Dismore, *15*

most single-season victories: Gilles Villeneuve, *9 (1976)*,
Patrick Carpentier, *9 (1996)*

most single-season victories from pole:
Gilles Villeneuve, *8 (1976)*,
Patrick Carpentier, *8 (1996)*

most consecutive victories: Patrick Carpentier, *8 (1996)*

most consecutive victories from pole/single season:
Patrick Carpentier, *8 (1996)*

most consecutive poles: Patrick Carpentier, *8 (1996)*

most career poles: Steve Shelton, *14*,  Gilles Villeneuve, *14*

most single-season poles: Gilles Villeneuve, *9 (1976)*

most money earned/single season: Patrick Carpentier, *$226,500 US (1996)*

most points earned/single season: Patrick Carpentier, *239 (1996)*

fastest qualifying lap:
oval: *156.32 mph/251.57 km-h*, Greg Ray, Nazareth Speedway (1994)
road: *128.15 mph/206.24 km-h*, Russell Spence, Watkins Glen (1992)

fastest race lap:
oval: *155.49 mph/250.24 km-h*, Patrick Carpentier, Nazareth Speedway (1995)
road: *126.50 mph/203.58 km-h*, John Lloyd, Watkins Glen (1987)

fastest race average speed:
oval: *144.34 mph/232.29 km-h*, Harald Huysman, Nazareth Speedway (1992)
road: *124.63 mph/200.57 km-h*, Calvin Fish, Watkins Glen (1987)

longest race:
*one hour, 7 minutes, .264 seconds; 47.4 miles*
Alexandre Tagliani, Grand Prix of Long Beach, Long Beach, CA (1997)

shortest race:
*22 minutes, 43.026 seconds; 50 miles/80.5 km*
Greg Ray, Milwaukee Mile (1994)

< 211 >

## LAP RECORDS THROUGH 1997 SEASON

| CIRCUIT | DRIVER | CHASSIS | TIME | mph | DATE | TEAM |
|---|---|---|---|---|---|---|
| **GRAND PRIX OF MIAMI** *(1.4-mile/2.25-km oval/road circuit)* | | | | | | |
| QUALIFY | Chuck West | Ralt RT-41 | 0:41.564 | 121.25 | 3/97 | World Speed Motorsports |
| RACE | Memo Gidley | Ralt RT-41 | 0:41.694 | 120.88 | 3/97 | Lynx Racing |
| | | | | | | |
| **TOYOTA GRAND PRIX OF LONG BEACH** *(1.59-mile/2.56-km street circuit)* | | | | | | |
| QUALIFY | Richie Hearn | Ralt RT-41 | 1:00.157 | 95.15 | 4/95 | Della Penna Motorsports |
| RACE | Jacques Villeneuve | Ralt RT-40 | 1:00.249 | 95.01 | 4/93 | Forsythe-Green Racing |
| | | | | | | |
| **NAZARETH SPEEDWAY** *(1.0-mile/1.61-km oval)* | | | | | | |
| QUALIFY | Greg Ray | Ralt RT-41 | 0:23.029 | 156.32 | 9/94 | Genoa Racing |
| RACE | Patrick Carpentier | Ralt RT-41 | 0:23.152 | 155.49 | 4/95 | Lynx Racing |
| | | | | | | |
| **MILWAUKEE MILE** *(1.0-mile/1.61-km oval)* | | | | | | |
| QUALIFY | Paul Jasper | Ralt RT-41 | 0:25.187 | 142.93 | 5/96 | B.D.J.S. |
| RACE | Patrick Carpentier | Ralt RT-41 | 0:25.067 | 143.61 | 6/96 | Lynx Racing |
| | | | | | | |
| **CIRCUIT GILLES-VILLENEUVE** *(2.69-mile/4.421-km road course)* | | | | | | |
| QUALIFY | Bertrand Godin | Ralt RT-40 | 1:38.687 | 100.20 | 6/97 | Player's/Forsythe Racing |
| RACE | Patrick Carpentier | Ralt RT-41 | 1:38.184 | 98.631 | 6/96 | Lynx Racing |
| | | | | | | |
| **MEDIC DRUG GRAND PRIX OF CLEVELAND** *(2.106-mile temporary airport road course)* | | | | | | |
| QUALIFY | Alexandre Tagliani | Ralt RT-40 | 1:09.197 | 109.56 | 7/97 | Player's/Forsythe Racing |
| RACE | Tony Ave | Ralt RT-41 | 1:10.162 | 108.05 | 7/97 | Olsson Engineering |
| | | | | | | |
| **MOLSON INDY TORONTO** *(1.784-mile/2.871-km street circuit)* | | | | | | |
| QUALIFY | Patrick Carpentier | Ralt RT-41 | 1:06.886 | 96.020 | 7/96 | Lynx Racing |
| RACE | Case Montgomery | Ralt RT-41 | 1:07.372 | 95.327 | 7/96 | Sandy Dells Racing |
| | | | | | | |
| **GRAND PRIX PLAYER'S de TROIS-RIVIÈRES** *(1.51-mile/2.42-km street circuit)* | | | | | | |
| QUALIFY | Jacques Villeneuve | Ralt RT-40 | 1:01.784 | 87.75 | 8/93 | Forsythe-Green Racing |
| RACE | David Empringham | Ralt RT-41 | 1:02.028 | 87.40 | 8/95 | B.D.J.S. |
| | | | | | | |
| **MID-OHIO SPORTS CAR COURSE** *(2.25-mile/3.62-km road course)* | | | | | | |
| QUALIFY | Jacques Villeneuve | Ralt RT-40 | 1:16.475 | 105.91 | 9/93 | Forsythe-Green Racing |
| RACE | Jacques Villeneuve | Ralt RT-40 | 1:16.319 | 106.13 | 9/93 | Forsythe-Green Racing |
| | | | | | | |
| **ROAD AMERICA** *(4-mile/6.44-km road course)* | | | | | | |
| QUALIFY | Chuck West | Ralt RT-41 | 2:03.611 | 117.89 | 8/97 | World Speed Motorsports |
| RACE | Chuck West | Ralt RT-40 | 2:06.059 | 114.23 | 8/96 | World Speed Motorsports |
| | | | | | | |
| **MOLSON INDY VANCOUVER** *(1.703-mile/2.74-km street circuit)* | | | | | | |
| QUALIFY | Memo Gidley | Ralt RT-41 | 1:03.833 | 96.044 | 8/97 | Lynx Racing |
| RACE | Alex Barron | Ralt RT-41 | 1:04.044 | 95.727 | 8/97 | Lynx Racing |
| | | | | | | |
| **LAGUNA SECA RACEWAY** *(2.238-mile/3.6-km road course)* | | | | | | |
| QUALIFY | Alex Barron | Ralt RT-41 | 1:18.755 | 102.30 | 9/97 | Lynx Racing |
| RACE | Patrick Carpentier | Ralt RT-41 | 1:19.696 | 101.52 | 9/97 | Lynx Racing |

< 213 >